BATIK
NEW LOOK AT
AN ANCIENT ART

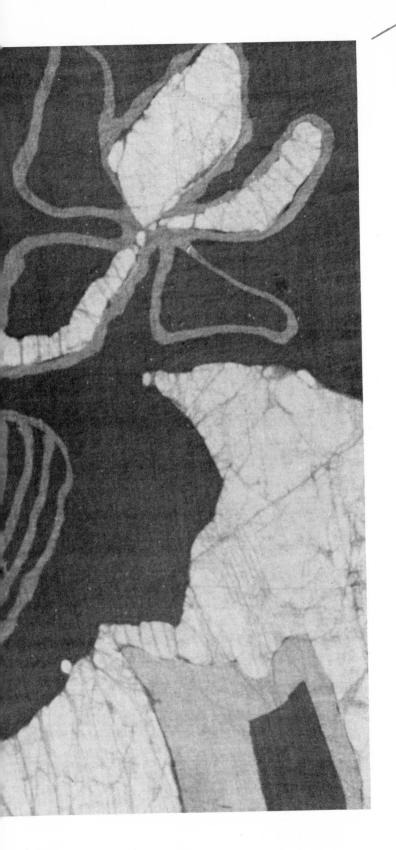

BATIK :

NEW LOOK AT AN ANCIENT ART

ROBIN AND JENNIFER SHAW

DOUBLEDAY & COMPANY, INC.
GARDEN CITY, NEW YORK
1974

We would like to thank Lynn Solow, our photographer

Book design by Mary Frances Gazze
ISBN: 0-385-01946-7
Library of Congress Catalog Card Number 72–89677
Copyright © 1974 by Robin and Jennifer Shaw
Printed in the United States of America
First Edition

To Janet and J. Harry

CONTENTS

8   INTRODUCTION

12   TOOLS AND MATERIALS
            The Tjanting   *14*
            The Brush   *16*
            Wax   *18*
            The Fabric   *18*
            The Wax Pot   *20*
            Dyes   *22*
            Dye Bath   *22*
            Removal of the Wax   *23*

24   COLOR AND BATIK
            The Color Circle   *25*
            Browns   *26*
            Harmonies   *26*
            Intensity   *27*
            Yellow   *27*
            Color Combinations   *27*
            Impossible Combinations   *28*
            Dyeing Procedure   *29*
            Dyeing Times   *30*
            Monochrome Pictures   *30*
            Shading   *31*
            Bleaching   *31*
            Painting-on   *32*

34 A FIRST BATIK

42 DESIGN AND THE BRUSH

51 DESIGN AND THE TJANTING

72 THE DISPLAY OF BATIK

78 PROJECT IDEAS FOR BATIK
Simple Doll 78
Jointed Doll 80
Quilted Doll 81
Sausage-dog Draft Pillow 83
Hobbyhorse Head 84
Cushions 86
Room Dividers 87
Lampshades 90
Quilts 93
Costumes 94

95 DYEING CHART

96 SUPPLIES AND BOOKS TO READ

INTRODUCTION

Batik is a medium that lies on the boundary between art and craft. Of Eastern origin and believed to be about 2,000 years old, the craft probably reached Java around the tenth century. There batik became an important element of both the culture and the economy. With the invention of the tjanting, complexity and speed of production were encouraged and the craft became accessible to many. Commercial production of batik received another impetus with the development of the tjap, a copper block akin to a linocut with which wax could be applied with a constant pattern to a large area of cloth. This industry has continued to expand up to the present with a doubling of the number of batik factories in the last decade to the astonishing number of 10,000. There has been a corresponding decline in inventiveness and craftsmanship.

The interest in batik in the West is of comparatively recent origin and resulted initially from Dutch trading contact with Indonesia. Modern interest has been focused mainly on batik as a craft medium, though recently artists such as Ila Keller and Joe Almyda have begun to extend the frontiers of the art. In 1971 a Society of Batik Artists was formed in New York and held its first show at the Community Art Gallery where more than fifty artists exhibited.

The technique of batik is a demanding one. In general, the final design must be conceived before the picture is begun. The batik artist works intimately with color; if he wishes parts of his design to be light yellow, for example, all these parts must be waxed at the same time before any subsequent dyeing. He cannot isolate one part of his design and complete it before moving on to the others as an artist in oils or water color may; he must create his design in stages, each of which encompasses the whole picture.

Moreover the artist in batik must progress from a lighter color to a darker; he cannot begin again. When we add to this the fact that the wax he is applying to the fabric is a fluid, running substance that often appears to have a mind of its own, we realize that this is a highly satisfying, even if initially frustrating, medium to master. There is a slightly accidental quality to even the most highly planned batik that often gives the picture an added dimension of excitement and life.

A batik portrait of Robin Shaw.

Fiery mask.

The brush was the main instrument in producing this delicate batik of a swan.

The purpose of this book is to introduce the artist to the possibilities of batik as a medium for fine art. It limits itself to those techniques which enable the artist to translate an idea onto cloth, usually silk or cotton, using the tjanting or the brush. The book does not deal with the many other methods of wax resist or the production of designs using object printing, wax crayons, or blocks. We encourage those readers interested in the various craft processes of batik to consult the bibliography at the end of this book.

Our aim is to lead the reader through the techniques of using the brush and tjanting, to give him a familiarity with the materials of batik and to explore the possibilities and limitations of the tools and the medium. We hope this book will be an inspiration to the craftsman and enable him to find new, meaningful expression in batik.

TOOLS AND MATERIALS

The basic process of batik is a simple one. It consists of permeating an area of fabric with hot wax so that the wax resists the penetration of dye.

If the cloth we begin with is white, such as bleached cotton, linen, or silk, then wherever we apply hot wax that area will remain white in the final design. After the first waxing the fabric is dipped into a dye bath whose color is the lightest tone of those to be used. When the piece has dried, we see an area of white and an area of cloth that is the color of the first dyeing. Wax is now applied to those parts in which we wish to retain the first color, and the entire fabric is immersed in the second dye bath whose color is darker in tone than the first. This process is repeated until the darkest tone required in the final design has been achieved. When the fabric, now almost wholly waxed, has dried it is placed between sheets of absorbent paper and a hot iron applied. As the sheets of paper absorb the wax they are replaced by fresh sheets until the wax is removed. At this point the final design is seen clearly for the first time.

The tools and materials used in batik are simple, cheap and readily available.

Any tool that can efficiently transfer hot wax from a container to the fabric will serve to produce a design on the cloth when it is dyed. At the simplest level, a lighted candle can be used to distribute drops of melted wax on the fabric. A variety of objects such as bent wire or the rim of a tin can, can be dipped in melted wax and pressed onto the cloth to make a design. Native producers of batik on a commercial scale use a copper block to obtain a repeat pattern on cloth.

However, for any serious artist in batik there are only two tools versatile enough to give control over the final design—the tjanting and the brush.

Batik tools: brushes of different sizes, a stylus-type tjanting and bowl-type tjanting.

The Tjanting

The tjanting is the traditional tool and is still widely used in Ceylon and Indonesia.

Essentially, it is a metal reservoir that holds the wax and a spout which allows the wax to be transferred to the fabric. Tjantings come in all shapes and sizes and though many are available few are very well designed. It is important to choose one carefully as a poor tjanting will be difficult to use, will make your initial attempts frustrating, and frequently will ruin a potentially fine design.

When buying a tjanting here are the qualities to look for:

1. The reservoir should not be too small. The essence of using the tjanting is to achieve flowing lines. If one is having constantly to return the tool to the wax pot, the rhythm is interrupted. Moreover the free-flowing qualities of the wax depend on its remaining above a minimum temperature. A tjanting with a large reservoir will generally retain its heat longer than a smaller one and, consequently, will allow the wax to flow for a longer time.

2. Where possible, the reservoir and spout should be of one casting so there is an even transfer of heat throughout the tool. Failing this, the jointing should be of good quality.

3. The spout should come from the bottom half of the reservoir. In this location it will be adequately heated by the wax. Some tjantings are available with the spout directly below the reservoir. While these do allow the free flow of wax and hold a considerable amount, they are very difficult to use. Obviously, the moment one lifts the tjanting from the pot the flow begins. It is necessary to hold some absorbent paper or cloth below the spout to stop the flow as the tjanting is carried to the start of the design on the fabric. Moreover, when one is executing the design it must be in a sure and unhesitating manner. Lifting this tjanting off the fabric is also hazardous and must be done quickly with the attendant risks of splashes of wax reaching areas of the design where they are not wanted.

These difficulties are common to all tjantings, but if the wax can be tipped away from the spout immediately, as is possible in the best tools, then the problem is minimized.

We have found that the only sure way to use the tjanting described above is to allow the wax in the reservoir to cool so that it runs from the spout in a slow rather than rapid trickle. However, this type usually also has a very open reservoir, and we have spoiled a few designs by slopping hot wax over the lip as the spout caught on the fabric.

4. Where possible, a variety of tjantings—each with a different spout bore—should be acquired. Where the spout is too narrow the wax will not flow freely, and where it is too wide the molten wax will gush. Between these dimensions there exist several possibilities, and your work will be more versatile if you possess a range of three or four.

Regrettably, many of the tjantings sold by arts and crafts shops do not appear to have been tested before marketing. Some do not work at all—for example, where the spout is positioned above the reservoir—and some work poorly. Choose carefully.

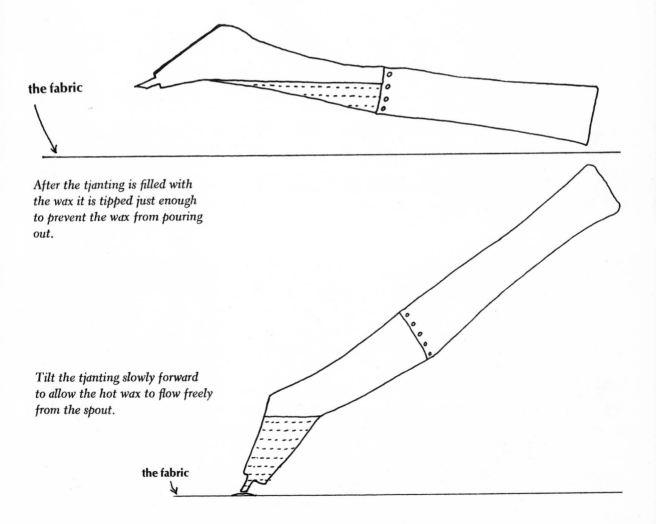

the fabric

After the tjanting is filled with the wax it is tipped just enough to prevent the wax from pouring out.

Tilt the tjanting slowly forward to allow the hot wax to flow freely from the spout.

the fabric

The Brush

The other essential tool for the batik artist is the brush. The best to use is about a number twelve water color. The brush needs to have a large enough tip to retain a good quantity of wax. If the tip is too small, what wax there is cools off so rapidly that it does not permeate the fabric adequately.

A larger brush for waxing out large areas of cloth is very useful as is a small brush—a number six is about as small as one can use—for delicate work.

Since the brush is subject to heat and fairly rough usage,

Using the brush to wax the outlined areas in seascape.

a good-quality brush is advised. The tip should be firmly connected to the handle. Having obtained a good brush, take care of it. If it is left in the wax pot when you are finished it will lose shape, the tip will loosen and it will be difficult to use.

Batiks produced using the brush possess quite a different quality and atmosphere from those produced with the tjanting. Design for both these tools will be dealt with in later chapters. At the moment it is enough to say that the tjanting is more suited to the production of pattern while the brush is better adapted to the creation of pictorial motifs.

Wax

The selection of waxes is important to the quality of the finished batik, though not as vital as is generally thought.

Paraffin wax and beeswax are the two waxes most commonly used in batik, and usually they are combined in different proportions to achieve different effects. The batik wax sold in art shops is usually a mixture of three parts paraffin wax to one part beeswax. It is advisable to obtain both kinds of wax and vary the proportions yourself.

Paraffin wax is more apt to crack than beeswax and should, therefore, be used in areas where more crackle is desired. With paraffin wax a dye bath up to a temperature of 90° F. can be used.

Beeswax is more supple than paraffin wax and can be immersed in a dye bath up to about 110° F. The cracks produced in the final design in areas waxed with pure beeswax are much finer. If you wish an area to retain a strong unbroken color through subsequent dyeings, then you should use pure beeswax on the fabric.

Though the mixture of waxes is important, the production or prevention of cracking can be obtained in other ways, such as the controlling of the dye temperature or the handling of the fabric, which will be dealt with later.

The Fabric

Because of its cheapness and availability, the best fabric for most batiks is cotton. A bleached bed-sheeting cotton about eighty inches wide is ideal. The weave of the cloth should not be too close, and the fabric should be translucent when held in front of a light. A heavier cotton will give more body to the finished work but will, in general, resist the wax and the dye to a greater extent.

Silk is the finest batik material because of its texture and suppleness but can be both difficult to obtain and expensive.

The artist should experiment with other materials as many different effects can be achieved with different fabrics. Natural fibers are by far the best as the artist is limited to a cold-water dyeing process, which is not suitable for most synthetic fabrics.

For the best results, the fabric to be waxed should be stretched on a frame, such as that used for canvas, and held in position with thumbtacks. The material must be taut to prevent wrinkles which may impede the free movement of the tjanting or cause the hot wax to run in an unpredictable way. The fabric may also be tacked to a board covered with paper or polyethylene sheeting. In this case, the back of the fabric must always be inspected, after its careful removal from the board, for areas that have not been fully permeated with the wax.

A fabric stretcher or canvas stretcher can be purchased in almost any art supply store.

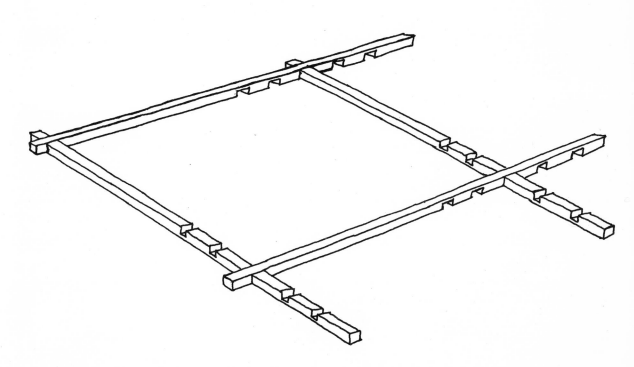

The Wax Pot

The wax pot is essentially a double boiler with the wax in a container sitting in boiling water. Perhaps the cheapest and most effective way to achieve this is to buy a corn popper and to use a clean can to hold the molten wax. If possible, the boiler should be large enough to hold two or more cans containing different proportions of paraffin and beeswax.

It is essential that the wax be close to the fabric as it must not cool on the brush on its way from the wax pot to the cloth. So the kitchen stove is not usually a suitable place to keep the wax hot.

Wax is an inflammable substance, so the wax container should not be placed directly on the source of heat. It should sit in boiling water, and care should be taken to see that the water is replenished as it evaporates.

Any double-boiler-type pan—in this case a popcorn popper—that is portable and can be handy to your working area is good to hold the wax containers.

Dyes

The most important point to remember in selecting dyes for batik is that they must be cold-water dyes. The waxed fabric cannot be placed in water that is more than tepid without the wax being melted out of the fabric with the consequent loss of the design.

Since the quality of the finished work depends to a great extent on the dye used, it is important to use dyes of a professional quality. The amounts of dye used are small. Therefore, there is little to be gained, even financially, in using a cheap dye. The dye may be used several times once it is mixed.

Among the best dyes available for batik are Perfection Dyes, Procion Dyes, and Chlorentine Dyes. Details of suppliers will be found at the end of this book.

As a minimum range of dyes to begin with, we would suggest canary-yellow, gold, pink, scarlet, dark brown, green, olive-green, turquoise, blue, purple, and black. By decreasing or increasing the concentrations of these dyes, or by combining them, one can produce an adequate range.

Dye Bath

Any shallow flat receptacle such as a roasting pan or a photographic tray will serve as a dyeing vat. Since the fabric is stiffened with wax, in general, one can only produce a finished work about twice the area of one's vat. Even this necessitates the folding of the fabric which may introduce undesired cracking, so it is best to acquire several vats of different sizes, which will enable one to lay the work in progress into the dye without folding, unless folding is desired.

The fabric is immersed in the dye then removed, rinsed in cold water and hung. If hung in such a way as to discourage wrinkling, subsequent work on the piece will be easier.

After the dyeing process the vat should be washed if it is metal since most dyes are corrosive.

Color theory applicable to batik dyeing and refinements in the dyeing and handling process will be dealt with at greater length in a later chapter.

Removal of the Wax

The wax can be removed in several ways. Some sources recommend boiling the fabric in water. The wax will melt and float to the surface of the water where it can be collected and reused. We do not feel that this is a suitable method in the production of fine art batiks since a loss of intensity in the color will result from boiling the piece.

A better method, we feel, is first to remove most of the wax by ironing the fabric between sheets of absorbent paper and then, if desired, dry cleaning it. Newspaper will be adequate for this job, and is less expensive to use than other absorbent papers, such as paper towels, but it should be at least a month old, otherwise the ink may be transferred to the batik.

The ironing process is a fairly slow and laborious one in which the fabric is placed on several sheets of absorbent paper with a single sheet covering the waxed areas. A hot iron is then applied on top of this sheet and the heat melts the wax which is then absorbed by the paper. When the top sheet is saturated with wax, it is replaced by a fresh sheet and the process repeated until most of the wax has been drawn from the fabric.

In this method, the cloth will never become wholly wax free. If the material is destined to be dress fabric, it should then be dry cleaned to return the original softness of the fabric, but if the piece is to be framed or hung, the artist may desire the somewhat stiffer quality caused by the residue of the wax.

When the wax is removed by ironing, it frequently spreads slightly on the fabric and darkens the surrounding color. This occurs where the fabric has not been wholly waxed, as is usually the case since there is no need to wax after the last dyeing. Consequently, the last-dyed area receives a darkening in certain parts. Frequently, this will produce a wax shadow which will add to the final creation and the artist may wish to retain this. If it is not desirable, the shadow can be eliminated either by the darkening of the entire area by the addition of cool wax and the application of a hot iron directly on the fabric; or, if desired, the wax can be totally removed by dry cleaning.

COLOR AND BATIK

As with painting, color is an integral part of batik. Without color there is no "painting"; without color there is no batik. A painter uses pigment; a batik artist uses dyes. Paint and dye differ from each other in many ways, and yet are also similar. The painter can, if he chooses, completely obliterate an undesirable color by covering it with another color. Perhaps he must wait until the unwanted color is dry, but there is no doubt about it, he has another chance; he can cover up his mistake.

In batik the correction of mistakes, in most cases, is impossible. The painter is not limited in any way in the variety of colors he uses and juxtaposes. In batik, however, each color used is significantly changed by the proceeding color; or at least it is certainly affected by the color "underneath." The only pure color is the first one, so all other colors used are mixtures, determined largely by the first color, or the first strong color. Because of this mixing there are many combinations of juxtaposed colors that are impossible to produce when using the true batik method (complete immersion of the fabric into the dye bath). There are other methods of dyeing that will give the artist greater scope for color combinations, and these will be dealt with further on.

Most of the possible color combinations can be seen in the dyeing chart on page 95.

The restriction on color combinations can be used to make batik distinctive. It is a built-in mechanism for producing combinations of harmonious colors, if certain pitfalls are avoided in choice of colors. These pitfalls are combinations of colors that produce muddy browns. Brown can be made in numerous ways, as a little experimentation with a box of water colors will prove. The following notes on color are designed to be particularly relevant to batik.

Dent Village in England. A monochromatic batik dyed in shades of gray and black.

24

The Color Circle

The simplest way of thinking about color is in terms of the color circle. Red, blue, and yellow are the primary colors, from which the other colors can be created by mixing. Orange, purple, and green are the secondary colors and are made by mixing the two primaries on either side, together, in equal proportions. Hence, yellow and blue will give green; yellow and red will give orange; red and blue will give purple.

The small triangles of color, situated between each primary and secondary are the sub-secondary colors. They are made by mixing the primary and secondary on either side, together, in equal proportions.

Browns

As mentioned above, one of the common hazards in dyeing is that after the use of only two or three colors, the fabric becomes a brownish color, which is usually muddy and undesirable. So it is useful to be aware of the many combinations that can make brown.

First of all, two secondary colors when mixed together will give brown. So this gives three possibilities—orange with green, green with purple, and purple with orange. The resulting brown in each case is slightly different.

When a primary color is mixed in equal proportions with the secondary color directly opposite to it on the color circle the resulting color will be brown. This gives three more combinations—red with green, blue with orange, and purple with yellow. It is the equal proportions that give the brown. A strong red with a weak green will give a muddy red rather than a brown.

It is important to remember that it is not necessarily the actual dye colors that will give the brown. If red, yellow, and blue are the dyes, the first color will dye the fabric red, but the second color will dye it orange. Then orange with blue will go brown. (This is not necessarily undesirable, but it is better if it is expected.) So the two colors to be thinking about are the color the fabric actually is and the color of the next dye, rather than the actual dyes already used.

Harmonies

It is possible to prevent deterioration of the purity and vividness of the color by using hues that are closely related on the color circle. Such closely related colors are usually referred to as harmonies. So, for example, a possible range for one batik would be: pale yellow, orange, and then deep red. Other possibilities include pink, mauve, and purple; lime, green, mustard green, and brown; and pale blue, violet, and dark blue.

Intensity

There is a need to progress from the least intense or lightest color to the deeper, darker colors. So, for example, if yellow, which is the lightest, least intense of all colors, is required to be in the picture, then yellow should be used first. Red and blue, two colors of equal intensity if pure and undiluted, and if they are both to be used in a batik, one must be chosen to be the "pure" first color. Whichever one is used second will be diluted and changed by the first. It is impossible to achieve a red and a blue both of full intensity in the same picture. However, by using a diluted first color it is possible then to use an intense second color, and the loss of intensity of this second color will be minimized. So a pale pinky-red can be covered by a strong blue and the blue will retain most of its character, and a pale blue can be covered by an intense red with only a little tingeing towards purple.

It is possible to use a very limited range of dyes to produce a wide variety of colors, just by varying the intensity or strength of the dye bath. For example, using just blue and red it would be possible to combine them in such a way as to finish with a four-colored batik. (See color section.)

Yellow

If yellow is required in a picture, it must be used first because it is the most easily contaminated color. However, yellow has the property of changing a number of other colors without losing the vividness of the original color. In this way yellow is used, although as a color itself it does not appear in the final picture. A picture dyed a brilliant pink, and dipped in a strong yellow will turn to a brilliant orange. An intense blue can be changed to a strong green, and a gray to a sage-green.

Color Combinations

As in all aspects of color, in relation to life and art, each individual develops likings for certain colors and certain color combinations. These are, in batik, arrived at through experimentation. It is a worthwhile practice to take notes on colors used, strength of the dye bath and dyeing times with each batik as it progresses. Each color is going to be changed by the colors underneath and after about three dyeings it is often impossible to say which colors, exactly, have been used, even when looking at the batik. In this way, pleasing combinations can be repeated with confidence of success.

The following list are some of the combinations we find ourselves using frequently:

  yellow, pink, scarlet, black
  yellow, chartreuse, gray
  pink, violet, blue
  chartreuse, primary blue, navy blue
  pink, magenta, purple
  orchid, pale blue, pink, navy blue
  pink, gray, blue, deep red
  orange, gray, blue

Impossible Combinations

In order to re-emphasize the color-combination properties of dyes, we are including here some notes on color changes that are not possible. These notes are based on experience as well as on the color chart and the color theories already discussed. Combinations that do not work are mainly the result of jumping about the color circle; taking a color from one side and then the other side and back to the original side.

It is impossible to have, for example, bright orange and bright blue together in the same picture (unless, of course, the dye is painted on). If the fabric is dyed orange first, then waxed and dyed blue, the piece will be orange and brown. If the fabric is dyed blue first, waxed and then dyed orange, it will be blue and brown.

Other such impossible combinations include green and red, purple and yellow, purple and green, orange and green, and purple and orange. Of course, the artist may still deliberately use these color combinations, with the purpose of making brown.

Dyeing Procedure

An appropriate quantity of dye powder is measured out. This quantity depends on the make of the dye, the amount of fabric, and the desired depth of color. If the dye is sold in sachets, it will probably be enough to dye one pound of fabric. So if the piece to be dyed weighs about one ounce, then about $\frac{1}{16}$ of the powder in the sachet should be used. If the instructions are for hot-water dyeing, the quantity of dye should be increased for cold-water batik dyeing. Check the instructions for the addition of salt, usually about one tablespoon of uniodized salt to a gallon of liquid.

The measured dye powder is mixed with about half a cupful of water, in a small pan, which is then heated until the dye particles have dissolved. Heating to boiling gives the most reliable results, but if very hot tap water is available, the dye will dissolve in this with extra time and stirring, and heating the water on an element can be omitted. Any undissolved particles will leave spots on the fabric. Clean cold water should be poured into the dyeing container—enough to cover the fabric easily—and then the dye solution should be added and stirred well to insure complete mixing and even distribution of the dye. Wetting the fabric in clean cold water before immersion in the dye guarantees even dyeing and is especially important when using heavy-quality cotton.

If the dye bath is cold water, this will encourage the wax to crack. Lukewarm water of about 80°–90° F. will keep the wax softer and will discourage cracking.

Complete, quick immersion of the fabric into the dye bath will avoid uneven dyeing. The fabric should be moved gently, or the liquid agitated in some way, such as tipping the bath a little and returning it to the horizontal. After a few seconds it is wise to withdraw a corner of the fabric to observe the effect. It must be remembered that the fabric will appear about twice as dark when wet than it will when dry. If a darker shade is then required, return the batik to the dye until the desired shade of color has been achieved. Remove the fabric from the dye bath either with gloved hands or tongs and rinse in lukewarm water (no hotter than 100° F.) until the water runs reasonably clear. The dye can be used again either to deepen the shade of this batik or for another one altogether.

The fabric now must dry thoroughly before it can be waxed again. Hang it up so that it will stay smooth and flat.

Dyeing Times

One color can be used to get a variety of results in one of two different ways. The dye can be mixed to give a very strong solution of color that will dye the fabric to the deepest possible shade for that dye. With this same dye solution, a number of lighter shades are possible by diluting the dye with extra water and thoroughly mixing. The more the dilution the lighter the resulting color. The other possibility, which can be used in conjunction with the previous one, is to vary the length of time the fabric stays in the dye bath. For the first dyeing the fabric may just be immersed in the solution and then taken out almost immediately. The second dyeing may last up to thirty minutes, and the third dyeing may involve leaving the fabric in overnight, thereby turning it the deepest possible shade for that one dye bath. All this would be in the same dye solution.

With the final dyeing it is possible to retain maximum fullness of color by omitting the rinsing stage. This is particularly useful when the final color is black and a dense black is required. It cannot be used before the last dyeing, however, because the surplus dye in the fabric will dilute and muddy the next dye solution used.

Monochrome Pictures

A monochrome picture with a variety of different shades can be achieved in one of two ways. A variety of dyes that generally come under the heading of one color can be used, progressing from the lightest to the darkest. Under the heading of gray, for example, there may be a pale gray, a greeny gray, a stone-gray and a dark gray. Under the heading of green there might be a chartreuse, a sage-green, a gray-green, and an olive-green. A picture that has undergone a succession of dyeings using those different grays will result in a predominently gray picture with certain shades looking cool and others looking warm. The Dent Village batik on page 25 was a progression through a variety of grays to black.

The second method, which results in a more truly monochromatic picture, involves the use of just one dye. The first dye bath is a weak solution, the second is made a little stronger by the addition of more dye powder, the third a little stronger still, and so on until the desired number of dyeings have been done. The Red Flower in the color section is an example of this technique.

It is, of course, possible to produce perfectly effective batiks by using only one color, and immersing the fabric in the dye only once. If the fabric was white to start with, the waxed design will be white, and all the rest of the fabric will be the one color.

Shading

By immersing the fabric in the dye bath and then very slowly lifting it out again, starting with one corner, or one side, a gradation of color can be achieved. The first section to be lifted out will be the palest. The last section to be lifted out will be the darkest. A possible specific use for this technique would be for a sky that is darker towards its zenith. It could also be used effectively in a non-representational picture to give extra emphasis to one area of the design.

Bleaching

Bleaching, a way of removing the color, can be used in batik to take out a color that has not created the desired effect, or to make way for a color combination that would not otherwise be possible. The area that is to retain its color must, of course, be waxed before bleaching. We have found this technique to be useful only to a limited degree because of certain drawbacks. Once a piece has been dyed it does not seem possible to entirely remove the color. The fabric usually becomes a yellowy color after bleaching, regardless of what color it was before. Also, after bleaching subsequent dyeings never seem to "take" quite as well; the colors are not as intense. However, with these limitations in mind it is possible, for example, to wax the cloth, dye it yellow, wax again, dye it red, then wax again. At this stage the colors not protected with wax could now be removed with bleach and the piece dyed blue. The resulting blue would be almost pure, instead of turning purple as it would have done if it was put on over the red. Another possibility for this technique is to use it for making the background color stand out in contrast to the rest of the colors. If the background color is not waxed in the early stages of the dyeing succession, but it is left until last, it may be undesirable to have such a possibly important area the muddy color, that often results from the combination of a large number of colors. Bleaching, and then redyeing may be an answer.

One consideration in the bleaching process is that the bleach will also reach into all those fine cracks and, if this is to be avoided, they must be waxed over carefully. Bleach penetrates the fabric more readily than dye. So if the wax is beginning to flake off or lift up from the fabric, the bleach will surely find these places unless the waxing is patched up It is important to rewax both sides of the cloth using very hot wax before the piece is bleached.

Painting-on

Intense and brilliant colors can be obtained using this technique, but that built-in guarantee of a harmonious combination of colors, that the dye bath technique gives, is absent. Any number of colors can be used in one batik, using this method. The areas to be painted need to be completely outlined in wax, even if only with a thin line. This line of wax acts as a boundary to prevent the wet dye from seeping along the cloth fibers into areas where that color is not wanted. A small quantity of dye solution is mixed up and is applied to the fabric with a soft brush. A number of applications can be made until the desired depth of color is achieved. This method does not lend itself to a uniform, even dyeing of larger areas, but small areas can be treated this way successfully.

A dye, other than the color you're working with, can be painted into special areas, like the eyes. Outline that particular area with wax, then paint on the color you want within that area. After it is dry, wax it to preserve the color, and continue with the normal dyeing process.

THE COLOR CIRCLE

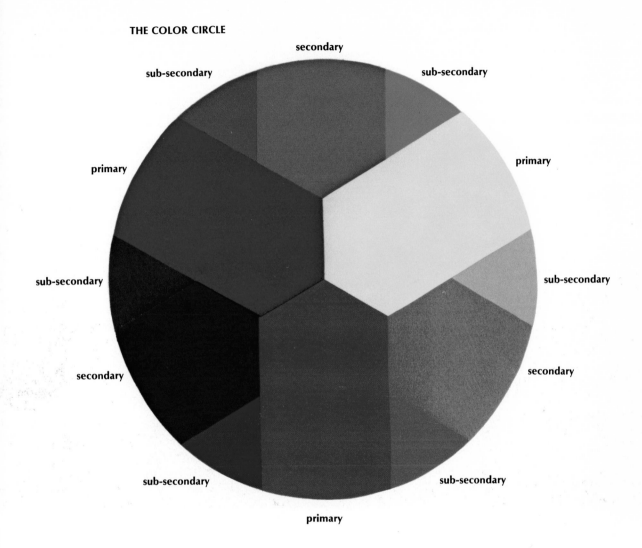

Using just two colors, blue and red, it is possible to finish with a four-color batik. The blue has been used twice, in the first box and in the last box with greater intensity; red was used in box 2 and 3 similarly.

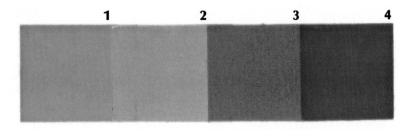

Mountain peaks.

Red Flower. A monochromatic batik in shades of red.

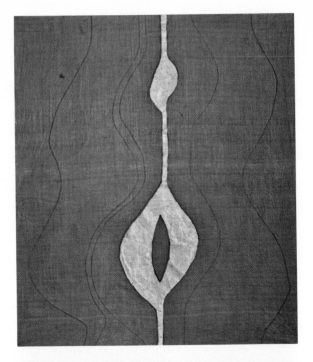

The area which it is desired to keep white is waxed and the fabric dyed magenta. (Left)

The area to be preserved as magenta is then waxed. Notice how the application of wax deepens the color. The fabric is then dyed navy blue. (Below left)

The purple area is then waxed (navy blue dyed over the magenta) and the fabric is dyed black. (Below right)

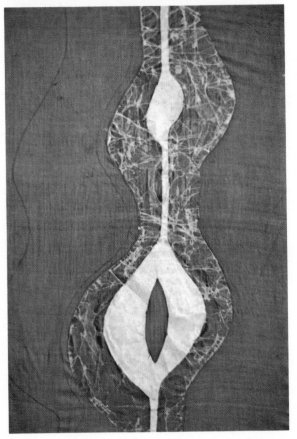

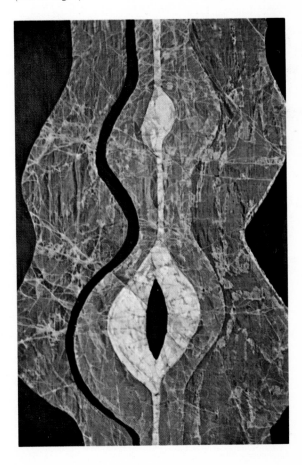

Batik ties in silk.

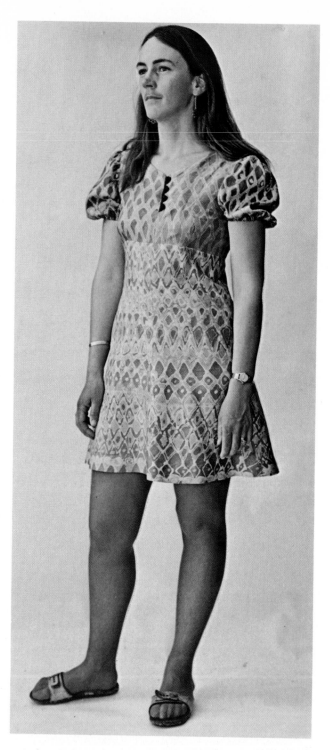

Batik cushion. The outlines were waxed freehand with a tjanting then a brush was used to fill in areas.

Batik silk dress. The skirt, bodice, and sleeves were dyed separately as pattern pieces and vary slightly in color and pattern.

A FIRST BATIK

In art as in life action is more important than words, so, having introduced the simple tools of batik, we will now set about producing our first creation.

For the first piece choose a design that is simple. Work with solid blocks of color covering a good expanse of fabric; opportunities for more delicate and accurate work will present themselves later.

Choose a design that will require few colors, perhaps three for a start. A design based on geometric forms, such as overlapping circles or squares, is ideal to begin with. Make your drawing simple, and confine yourself to drawing the outline as you sketch. When you are satisfied with the arrangement, transfer your idea to the cotton fabric.

To do this, stretch the fabric on a board, using thumbtacks to hold it in position, and then draw the design on it with a soft pencil or charcoal. Do not make your lines too heavy or they will be apparent in the final design.

Then stretch the fabric on a frame. If no frame is available, then fix the cotton on a board over newspaper or plastic sheeting, or alternatively on a sheet of thick cardboard. (See page 19.) The frame, though not essential, is advised as it allows an easy and uniform penetration of the wax. Make sure that your wax is thoroughly melted in the wax pot. You are now ready to begin waxing.

Decide which area of the final design you wish to be white and apply the wax to it using the brush. A mistake many beginners make is to try to cover too great an area with wax, before returning the brush to the pot to be reheated.

Look for the tell-tale translucence that the wax imparts to the fabric as you wax it. When the wax cools on the brush, it lies on the surface of the fabric without permeating it, and consequently does not form a good resist to the dye.

When the area to be white appears to have been waxed, turn the fabric over and check that the wax has penetrated thoroughly. If not, touch up the bare spots at this point.

The fabric is now ready for the first dyeing. Choose a fairly light color, mix the dye, and then dilute it in the dye bath with cold water. To be on the safe side, the dye should feel cold. If it is more than tepid, then the wax in the fabric

The log.

After the fabric is either stretched onto a fabric stretcher or tacked onto a board, the design is sketched lightly with a pencil.

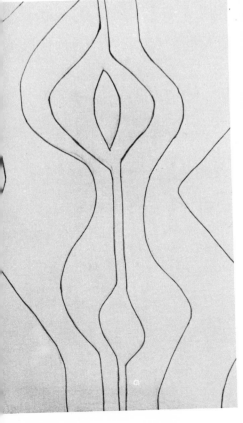

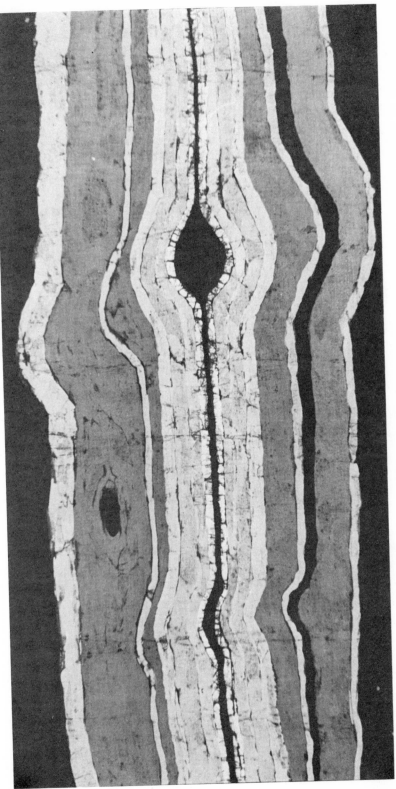

The area to remain the true color of the fabric is waxed first. Notice how the area looks darker, indicating the wax has permeated the fabric. (Below)

When the waxing is finished, turn the fabric over to check for dry spots where the wax did not penetrate to the back. (Opposite)

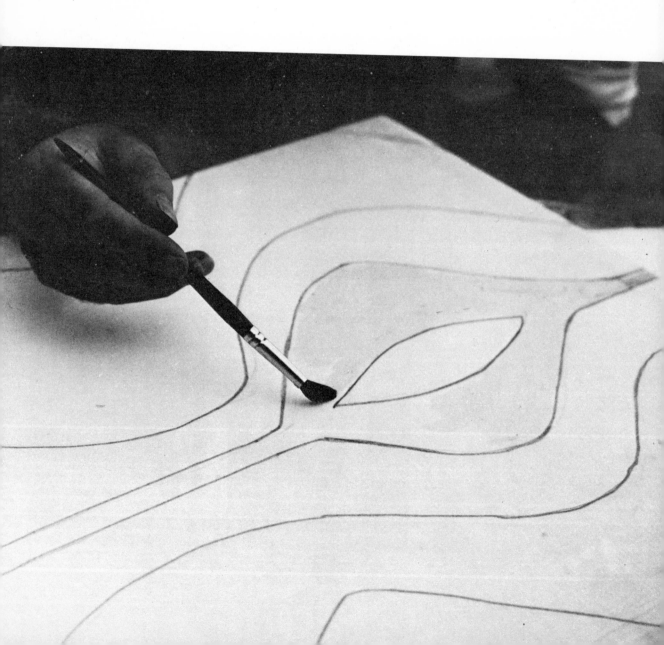

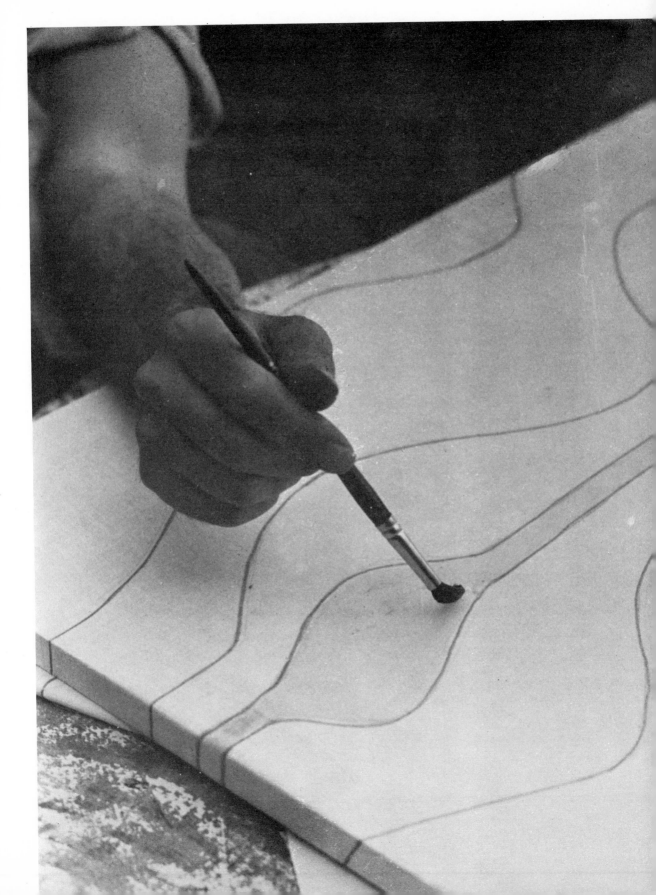

will melt and the design will be ruined. Many beginners make this mistake; once we spoiled a batik on the last of nine dyeings by using hot instead of cold water! There is nothing worse than watching a fine design dissolve before your eyes.

Remove the fabric from the waxing frame, handling it carefully to avoid undesired cracking, and immerse it in the dye bath. If you are unsure about the strength of the dye, then use a test strip of the same cotton, before you commit your piece to the dye bath.

When the fabric has taken on the desired color remove it from the bath and rinse it thoroughly in *cold* water.

Do not wring the piece but hang it up carefully and allow it to drip dry.

Remove the cloth carefully from the stretcher or the board and immerse it into the cool, or lukewarm, dye bath. A hot dye bath will melt the wax and ruin your batik.

The initial temptation in batik is to speed the process up. However, this leads only to unsatisfactory results. Any attempt to dry the fabric more quickly with artificial heat will usually result in the wax melting; waxing the fabric before it dries thoroughly will prevent the wax from permeating the fabric.

We find that the best way to inhibit impatience is to have three or four designs to work on at the same time. While the first piece is drying one can be waxing the others.

When the fabric is thoroughly dry stretch it on the frame again. You will see that there are two colors on the piece, the white cotton that received the first wax, and the color of the first dyeing. We now have to decide what areas

Notice how the waxed area remains white. Rinse it in cool water and hang it up to dry.

of that color we wish to retain and impregnate them with hot wax as before. As you wax that color, you will notice that its tone deepens as it is saturated with the wax. That is the tone it will be in the final design unless you remove the wax fully by dry cleaning, in which case it will be slightly lighter.

The second dye bath is now prepared. It must generally be a darker color than the first. The dyeing chart on page 95 will assist you in choosing the color.

After the fabric has been dyed, rinsed, and dried it is now ready for the final waxing and dyeing.

You will find that the earliest waxing, since it is subject to most handling and immersion in cold water, will be the most cracked. If it has not been rewaxed, you will, by now, find fine lines running through it, which have the color produced by the latest dyeing. If you wish to preserve the lines at that color, wax over the top of them with hot wax, the hotter the better for this purpose.

Once you have waxed out the areas that have to retain the color produced by the second dye bath, the fabric is dyed in the last color, which must again be darker than the previous one.

When the fabric has been rinsed and dried, the wax can be removed. This is an exciting moment, as only now does the total design, which has been obscured by the wax, emerge. Place the batik between sheets of an absorbent paper, such as old newsprint. You should have several sheets below the batik and a single sheet above. Apply a hot iron over the single sheet. You will see the wax being drawn out of the fabric into the paper. When the paper is saturated remove it, replace it with a fresh piece and repeat the process. It usually takes about six or seven sheets of newsprint to remove the wax. The batik is now finished, and you can see the colors in their full richness, with the blocks of color enlivened by fine lines of the other colors. Even a very simple design may produce a fine batik because of the quality which these fine lines, or crackle, produce.

Suggestions for displaying and mounting the batik will be found in a later chapter.

Once you have mastered the basic techniques and produced several simple designs, you will be ready to develop your techniques to cope with more complex and intricate creations, some requiring as many as ten dyeings.

Place the finished batik between several sheets of old newspaper on the bottom and one sheet on top. With a hot iron go over the batik until the paper is saturated with wax. Replace the top sheet as many times as necessary until all the wax is drawn out.

DESIGN AND THE TJANTING

The brush is the most versatile tool for batik. With it, one can produce a fine line or block out an entire area. Working with a brush and hot wax, most of the effects of oil painting can be achieved. The purpose of this chapter is to look at the kind of design that will best be executed with a brush, and to introduce some of the finer points of brush technique.

In an earlier chapter we dealt with the production of a simple batik in which we used the brush to block out substantial areas of the fabric with wax. It was only important in that batik to make sure that the wax was sufficiently hot, when it reached the fabric. By now it will be noticed that wax, unlike paint, does not remain where it is placed on the fabric. It has a tendency to creep along the threads of the fabric, and the hotter it is the farther will the wax penetrate. It is frequently difficult to predict how far the wax will spread; it may be up to one half an inch. Consequently, when you transfer the brush from the wax pot to the fabric, place it first in an area where spread will not be critical.

When waxing up to a line on your design, start your brush stroke about half an inch from the line, and move your

The sketch for a landscape design.

When waxing around a small area of the design that you would like to remain wax free, allow the wax to cool on the one side before waxing the other side. Otherwise the heat will draw the wax across the unwaxed portion.

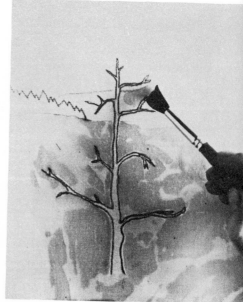

brush parallel to the line. The hot wax will spread through the fabric up to the line. When your brush is laden with hot wax the faster you move it on the fabric the less the wax will spread laterally.

Remember that the warmer your fabric is the more inclined the wax will be to spread. So, if you are waxing one area close to another that has just been waxed, such as on both sides of the tree in the winter scene, give the fabric time to cool. Otherwise, you may find that the wax you are applying will join up with the just-waxed area and obliterate the fine line you were leaving to be dyed between them.

Applying the wax with rapid movements of the brush will prevent the wax from penetrating fully, resulting in a mottled effect after dyeing. This has a nice subtle appearance for things like sand on the beach, or fields of snow.

Often as your designs become more complex you will
wish to wax a small area, such as the whites of the eyes in the
portrait. Here it is important that the wax does not spread
or the intended effect will be lost. In these cases it is best to
take a scrap of fabric and experiment with it. It may be best
to first dab your brush on a scrap before proceeding to the design, to remove most of the wax from the brush, but you
must be careful not to allow the wax to cool down too much.

A brush is used to wax large areas of a design. Crackling results when the wax doesn't permeate or doesn't cover the cloth entirely. When waxing a large area keep in mind that if the brush strokes run parallel to the design then the crackle, if it results, will be parallel also. If the brush strokes are at random, the crackling will be at random.

Beeswax flows less readily than paraffin wax, and it can be useful in a situation like this.

The brush, of course, can be moved quickly or slowly over an area carrying hot or cool wax to produce different effects. The faster the brush moves, the less the penetration.

An area waxed out, without thorough penetration of the wax, will allow dye to seep in usually from the back of the fabric and will produce a mottled effect. This can be used

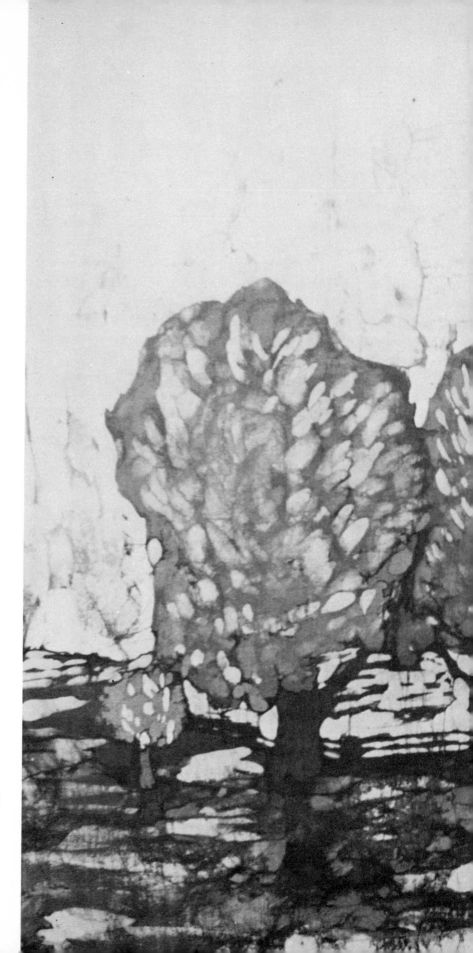

Short, close, but separate
brush strokes give a clustered
effect; for instance, leaves
on a tree.

when one is waxing out a large area where variety is desired, such as an area of sand or a snowy field. In these cases the wax is applied with rapid movements of the brush. Some areas will receive the wax fully while other areas will not be penetrated so completely. The result after dyeing will be a variegated expanse.

The brush can be used in short strokes, separated from each other, to give a broken and multicolored quality to an area, such as the foliage of a tree in autumn or a seascape.

When waxing a large area in this way it is important to consider the direction of the brush strokes. If, for example, the brush strokes are parallel to the bottom of the fabric, and the area is not completely permeated with wax, the crack lines will also be parallel to the base of the fabric. Using this technique it is possible to arrange the crack lines in the finished picture. The wax can be applied in straight or curved brush lines for different effects.

The limitations of batik are those of color, rather than tool. As familiarity with the brush and the flowing properties of waxes increases, the artist will find that he can produce works of great intricacy and delicacy.

In batik, as in oil painting, the subjects that the artist can deal with are only limited by his imagination. He can attempt naturalistic or abstract pictures. The most successful batiks appear to have the quality of motion, of being restless creations; so the sea or water makes an excellent subject.

The fine crackle produced in most batik, give to the picture a feeling of antiquity, so we have found that subjects from medieval art are particularly successful. So, also, are scenes reminiscent of the work of nineteenth-century impressionists, since batik softens hard lines, and the crackle gives a broken up atmosphere to blocks of color.

An excellent exercise is to select a painting by some artist you admire and attempt to reproduce it in batik. This will force you to use the brush in a way that demands fine technique. It will also expand your ideas of what can be achieved with the medium.

The crackling in the batik of St. George Slaying the Dragon gives it an antique look.

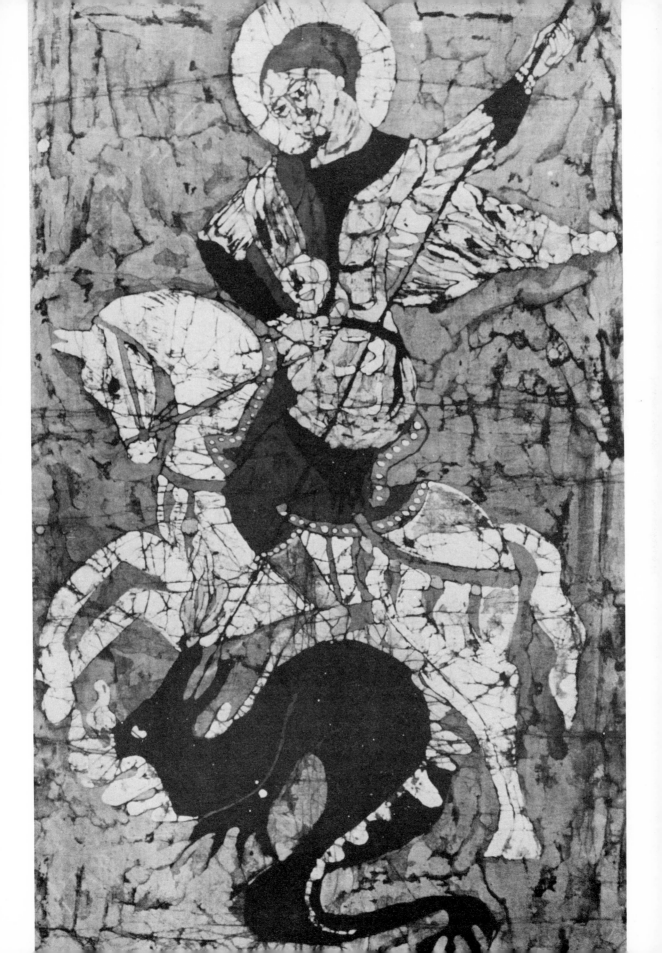

The coiled snake was designed with the tjanting.

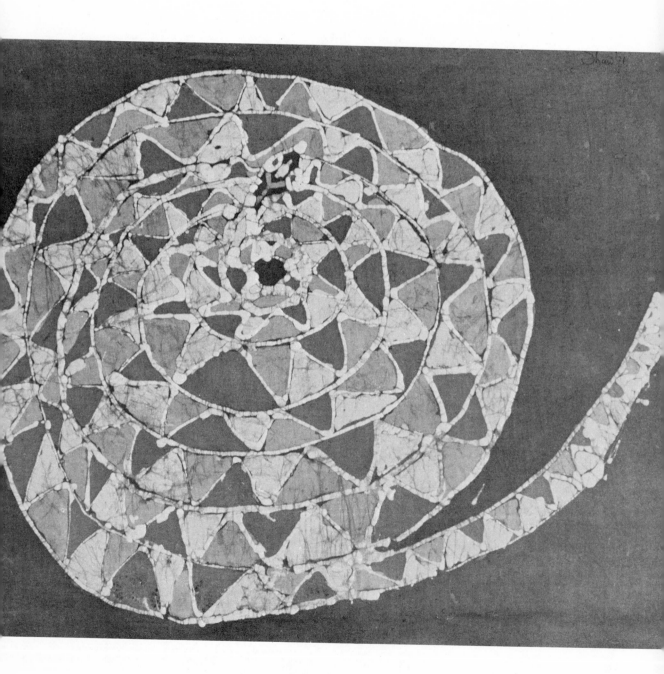

DESIGN AND THE BRUSH

Imagine a paintbrush with a continuous supply of paint flowing from its tip. When using a tjanting, one has in one's fingers such an instrument. As wax runs from the spout and penetrates the cloth, a line or area of color is being preserved through all subsequent dyeings. If one runs the tjanting over blue fabric, the area penetrated by the wax will remain blue.

Designs most suited for use with the tjanting are those with linear arrangements and patterns of intricate and delicate feeling. The essentials of form are sought and quick decisive lines are encouraged.

An inexperienced user should plan on a flowing simple line since, once the tjanting is placed on the cloth, it must be kept moving until it is removed. Most tjantings can, of course, be tilted to stop the flow, or the tjanting can be quickly lifted and the spout stopped with a wad of paper towel. The user quickly becomes accustomed to these movements but at first the usual result is to drip wax in unplanned areas. Even for the experienced user the avoidance of blobs where one begins and ends a movement is a difficult art. So begin with an uncomplicated flowing design. Plan to use the tjanting continuously until the reservoir of wax is empty or until the wax cools and stops flowing.

The fact that most tjantings hold so much wax lends itself admirably to continuous lines; unbroken lines that can be curved and flowing or angular. Angular lines are difficult to achieve with a constant thickness. There tends to be a slowing down or hesitation at the corner that causes the wax to form a blob. This blobbing, however, gives a particular effect of its own that can be used to advantage in a design. The more acute the angle of the corner, the more likely that a large blob will be produced, as there must be a greater hesitation at this point, and also the wax before the corner has heated the surrounding fabric causing the wax to flow more readily.

If the tjanting is held so that the spout is in contact with the fabric, and it is moved steadily, the line produced will be of constant thickness. If part of the line is to be thicker, the movement is slowed down, or speeded up if the desired line is to be thinner.

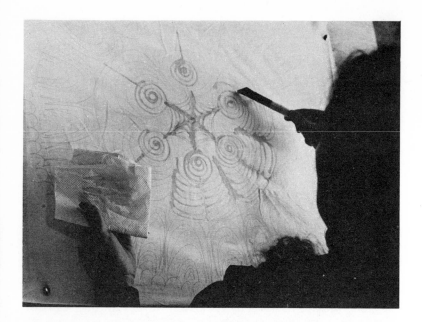

*Waxing over the sketch
with the tjanting. If the tjanting
cannot be tilted back to stop
the flow of wax, then keep folded
paper towels handy to put under
the spout and stop the flow of wax.*

*In the dye bath the waxed linear
design resists the dye solution.*

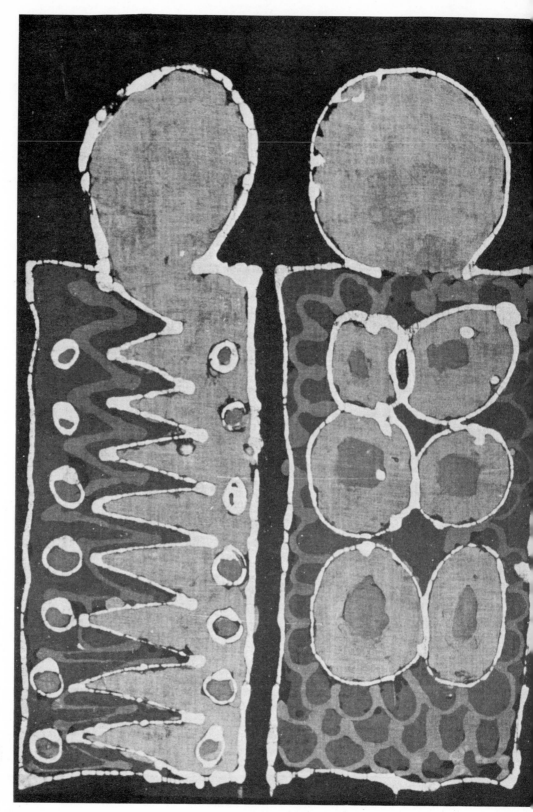

Candles.
When turning
corners with
the tjanting the
wax may blob
at the corner, an
effect that could
be incorporated
into the design.

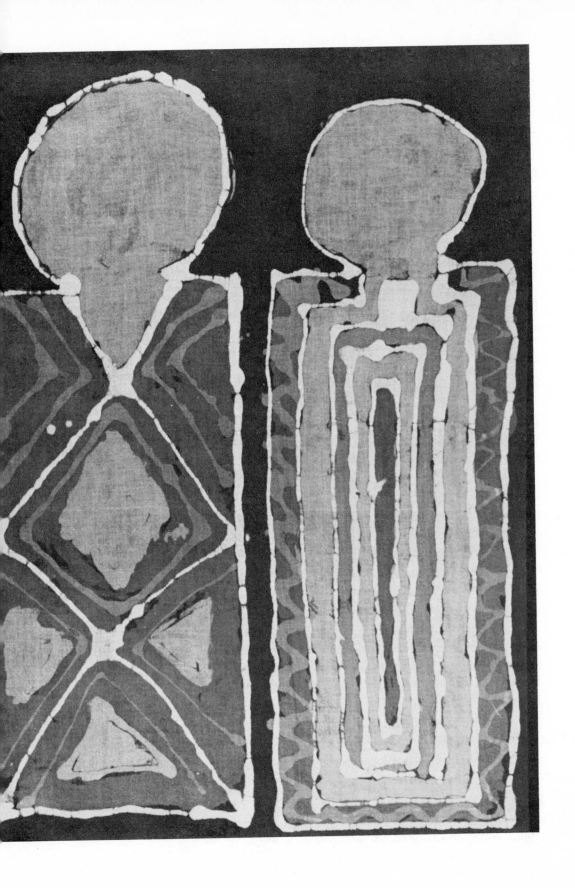

The temperature of the wax is an important controlling factor in the use of the tjanting. To fill the tjanting, the bowl is immersed in the hot wax in the pot so that the bowl fills up. It is then carried carefully to the point on the fabric where the waxing is to begin, with the spout tilted back and a paper wad held under it. At this point the wax is at its hottest and therefore most free flowing. As the waxing progresses and the wax cools, it gradually becomes less liquid and emerges from the spout more slowly. So, to keep a line of constant thickness, there are two alternatives. The first is to move the tjanting fairly fast at first, gradually slowing to correspond to the viscosity. The second alternative is to allow the wax to cool a little before beginning the line and then the change in speed required is reduced to the minimum.

In addition to lines, the tjanting can be used to produce other effects.

If the tjanting is lifted above the fabric and moved faster than the flow can produce a continuous line, then an irregularly broken line will result. In this position if it is moved more slowly, the line will have irregular areas of thickness like knots in a string. Using a variation of this technique, the tjanting can produce dots or spots of varying size on an area of the fabric. For the consistent production of dots, it is almost essential to have a tjanting that can be quickly tipped back to stop the flow of wax. For this effect the tool should be held very close to the fabric and almost horizontal. In this position a very slight change in angle will cause the wax to start and stop flowing, and the amount of wax emerging can be controlled fairly easily. It will help also in this technique if the wax is fairly cool so that it does not penetrate a large area of cloth.

Familiarity and confidence in this technique enables the artist to produce effects akin to pointillism. Dots placed very close together, however, will never quite totally cover the area. This is especially so if they are placed on the fabric at different times. Each dot will be surrounded by a very fine line of unwaxed fabric. Consequently, unless the whole area of dots is waxed over with a brush these minute lines will continue to darken as the fabric goes through the series of dye baths. Very fine effects are produced using this technique.

If the spout of the tjanting is pressed very firmly against the fabric this, too, will stop the flow of wax. Because of

To produce the effect of pointillism, the tjanting is held very close to the fabric, almost in a horizontal position, and can be tipped back quickly to stop the flow of wax.

this, another technique is possible—one reminiscent of the path a snail deposits on a leaf, except that in the case of the snail no part of the leaf appears untouched! This method is one way of using the tjanting to cover an area of the cloth that occupies more space than the line.

The spout is pressed firmly on the fabric and moved slowly along. At some point the tjanting runs parallel and adjacent to a previous line and moves along it, the new line touching the old one without overlapping it. The area, when finished, is filled in with wax lines. When the fabric is dyed, fine lines of dye penetrate the threadlike area between the lines, while the waxed line remains the color of the previous dyeing.

The tjanting can also be used to produce many "realistic" effects. Forms from nature that lend themselves to the use of the tjanting include trees, ferns, snakes, grasses, spider webs, and ripples on water. In general, however, the tjanting does not lend itself to realism. The artist in batik may use it, how-

Abstract geometric design.

The Feather Ring. Linear designs lend themselves especially well to the tjanting.

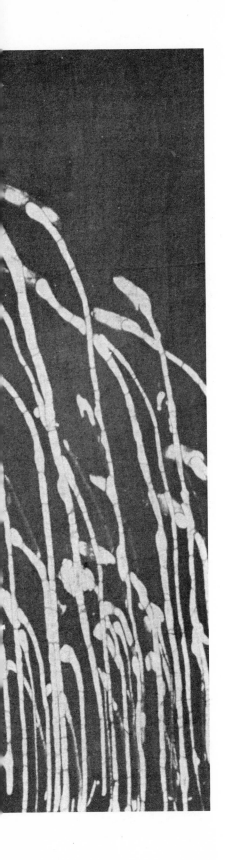

The tall grass was made with
a tjanting moving from the top
downwards off the edge of the
batik. Notice the blobs where the
full tjanting lingered a second
longer.

The tjanting can be used to
produce a special effect in an
otherwise brush design.

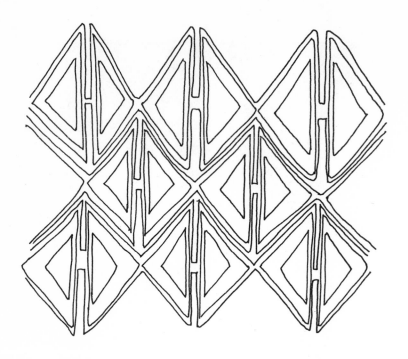

Geometric design.
Even the repetition of a variation
of the letter of the alphabet would
work well with the tjanting.

Hexagon design.

ever, to produce special effects in an otherwise brush-waxed picture.

The tjanting is highly suited to the production of linear designs both abstract and representational. To follow the idea of abstract designs, the geometric pattern has endless possibilities. The circle can be treated singly as an area into which patterns can be fitted, or a number of interrelated circles can be arranged so that the shapes in between are the connecting idea. The square also can be used in this way. The brick effect and the half-drop effect become easily applicable to the square. The triangle, diamond, and the hexagon, all related

Scale design.

shapes, give interesting combinations when fitted together. The ogee and the scale are also possible bases for the formulation of a pattern design.

The repeat of a shape always has small variations, which produce soft and individual effects. The pattern may be a small part of a predominantly brush batik; it may be used to give shape to a figure, or texture to a house or tree. The artist may start by drawing the shape with the tjanting then patterning areas of the shape in later dyeings. The necessity for executing the lines of the figure in smooth uninterrupted motion impose on the artist the need to isolate the essentials of the form he wishes to create.

Many of the American Indian figure and pattern drawings are excellent inspiration material for the linear effects suited to the tjanting. The same applies to many primitive art forms, especially African art. Traditional Indian art is also very decorative, and many Indian sculptures and jewelry designs can be adapted to the batik medium.

The Bayeux Tapestry and other medieval pictures can be translated into tjanting designs. A collection of antique keys or a brass rubbing of an old church brass often have minute details and distinctive intricacies that can be utilized for this tool.

In many designs it may be advantageous to use the tjanting in conjunction with the brush. A child's alphabet, for example, can be done by using the tjanting for the letters and the outline and pattern of the illustrations. Then the brush can be used to fill in the shapes or the background, to give a differentiation through color. There are many childhood themes that could be treated in this way. Noah's Ark, a number chart, a zoo, and the Kangle Wangle's Hat are a few such themes.

Modern artists in batik have tended to shun the tjanting in favor of the brush as the effects that can be produced by the latter are more predictable and less "accidental." While this is true, the technique of the tjanting, when mastered, can be used to produce batiks that are unique in their atmosphere and feeling. Moreover, to use the tjanting is to place oneself on a technological level with the Javanese craftsman and to instill an understanding of and a great respect for his creations, while opening up a wealth of artistic possibilities which cannot be tapped with a brush.

Diamonds.

64

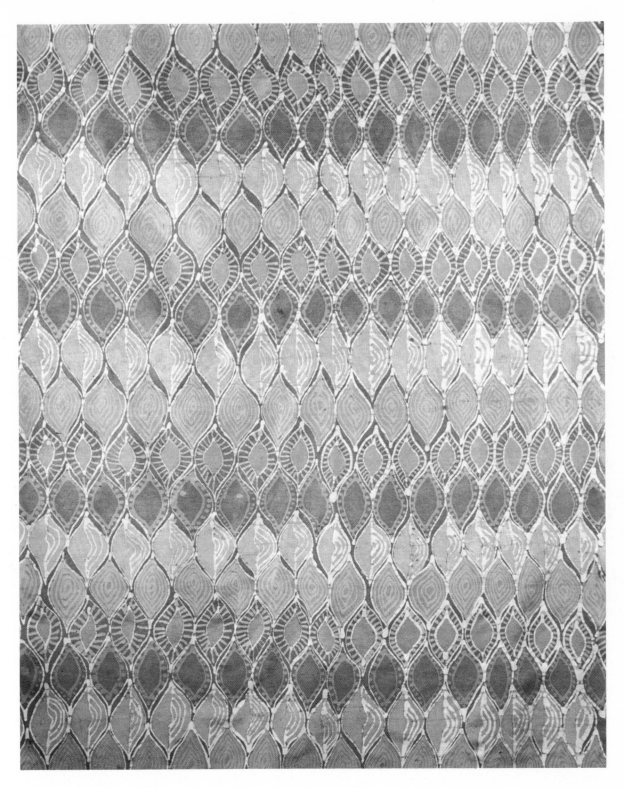

Length of silk dyed first a strong yellow, then orange, and finally red.

A Vermont fall scene.

Batik after a self-portrait by Pissaro.

The sun behind the grasses. The fine crack lines produced by batik lend themselves to realistic possibilities. (Below)

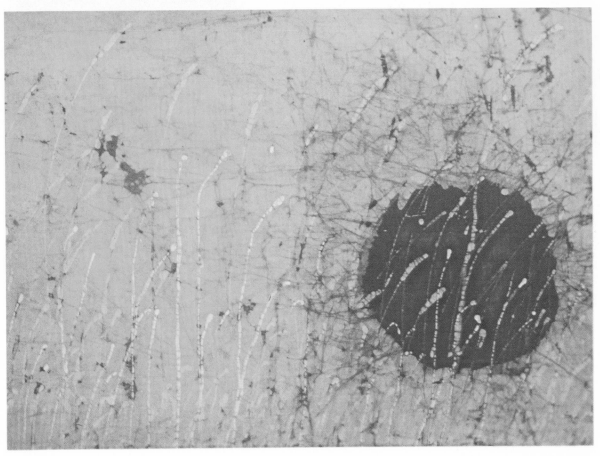

Seascape.

The square—half drop.

Ogee design.

American Indian designs.

African designs.

Design of India.

African mask.

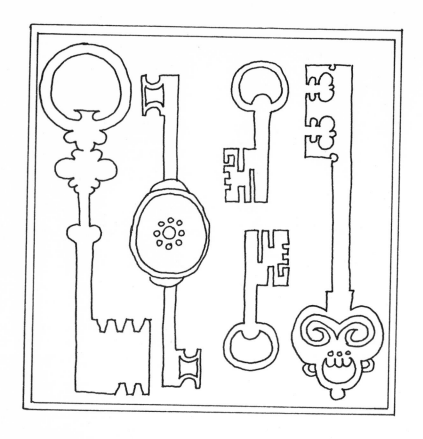

Antique keys.

Child's alphabet.

THE DISPLAY OF BATIK

When the wax has been removed from the fabric, the batik is now ready to be mounted. This is an important part of the process; too many fine pieces are not seen at their best because of inferior mounting. Frequently you will find that the batik gains considerably in interest and appeal from an effective display.

Unlike a painter's canvas, a batik has the design or picture on both sides. The first step is to choose the side you wish to display. Most often it will be the side you worked on, but occasionally the reverse side, which usually has had greater contact with the dye, will be the most attractive.

There are many ways in which to display the finished batik. Perhaps the simplest method is the wall hanging. The fabric should be hemmed with a wide hem at the top and bottom to allow a rod of wood or metal to be slid into the sleeves. Metal is best for this as its weight helps the batik hang properly when placed on the wall. The batik should also have a narrow hem on both sides. Cord or wire can be attached to the topmost rod.

One method of displaying a batik would be to slip a dowel through the top and bottom hem.

Some artists, notably Joe Almyda, feel that the finished batik should simply be fringed and hung on the wall where it will be free to move gently with air currents. If this is your wish, make a wide hem at the top of the batik and insert a rod from which the batik can be suspended. All other sides of the fabric should then be frayed to a depth of about a quarter of an inch.

Probably the most popular method of presenting a batik is to construct a simple frame of wood and then staple the fabric on to it. It is important, if you intend to display the batik by this method, to anticipate the edge of the fabric required to go round the frame when you are designing the batik.

In order to make the frame you need access to a few tools—a woodsaw, a miter block, and a staple gun.

Firstly, measure the finished batik and then allow about an inch and a half to two inches of fabric on each edge to go over the frame. For example, if the batik measures twenty-four inches by twelve inches, then the frame should be twenty-one inches by nine inches.

To construct the frame, then, four pieces of wood are required, two of them twenty-one inches in length, and two

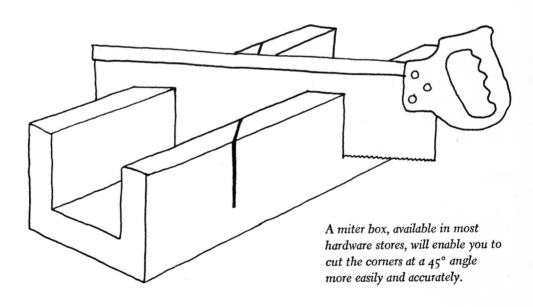

A miter box, available in most hardware stores, will enable you to cut the corners at a 45° angle more easily and accurately.

73

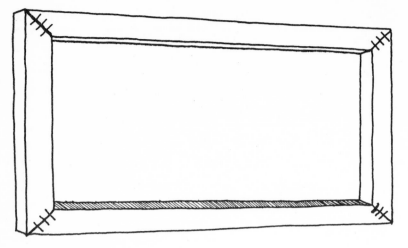

The mitered edges are fitted together, and then the corners are strengthened on both sides with staples.

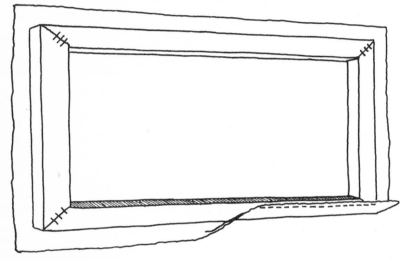

Stapling the first edge of the fabric to the readied frame.

nine inches in length. The wood should normally be about one inch thick. If you are constructing a frame for a larger batik, then the wood should be thicker, to prevent the frame from bowing under the tension of the fabric.

When the four lengths of wood have been sawed, the corners must now be mitered at a forty-five degree angle.

The four sides are now fitted together and a heavy-duty stapler is used to shoot about three staples into each corner on both sides of the frame. (The corners of the frame can be strengthened if wood joiners are used instead of staples.) The frame is now ready to have the fabric stretched on it.

Place the fabric with the side you wish to display face down on a table. Lay the frame over it and begin to staple an

Rest the frame on top of the batik and staple the top edge of the batik to the frame. Stretch and staple the opposite end of the batik to the frame. Do the same with the remaining sides.

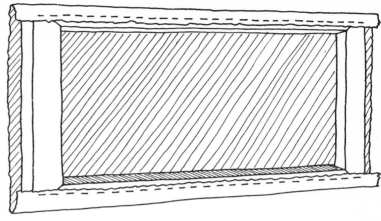

The corners should be folded and stapled like this.

Bookbinding tape or masking tape can be used to cover the raw edges. Picture wire is attached to the screws for hanging.

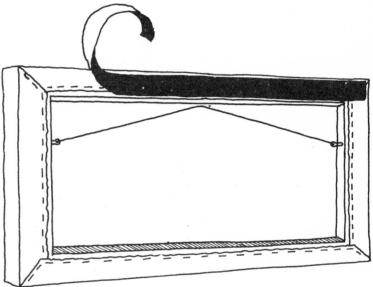

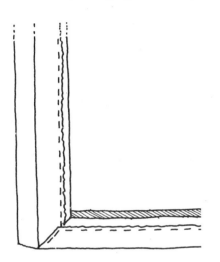

edge of the batik to the back of the frame. When one edge is stapled to the frame, the batik should be drawn tightly over the opposite side of the frame and again stapled to the frame. Repeat the procedure with the other sides of the fabric until the batik is stretched tightly over the frame.

Finish off each corner as shown and then trim off any excess fabric. The staples in the back of the frame should be covered with strips of masking tape.

To complete the frame for hanging, a hook should be screwed into each side of the frame and a length of picture wire attached to the hooks. The batik can now be hung on the wall.

Once this basic frame has been used to stretch the batik

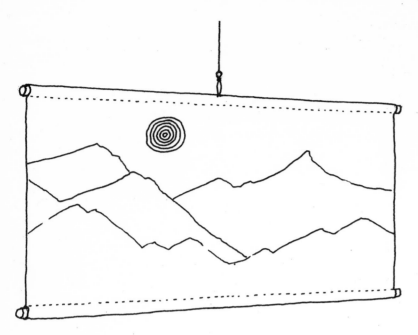

Hanging a batik in this manner will allow it to sway gently with the air currents.

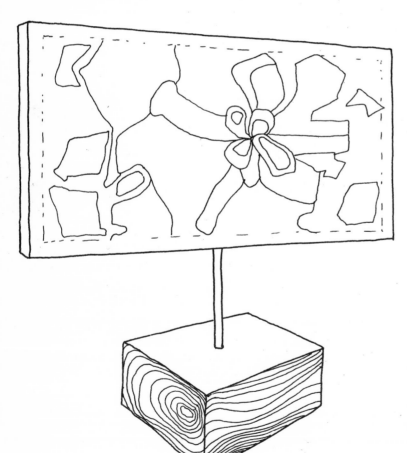

The mounted batik can be fastened onto a stationary object.

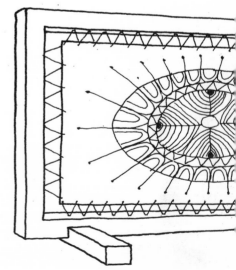

it can then be incorporated in a surrounding frame of wood or metal. Barn board makes a very attractive surrounding for some batiks, as does stainless steel.

In general, the batik is best displayed without a surrounding frame which can often detract from the delicacy of the finished work. Also, it is usually a mistake to cover the batik with glass, as this inhibits the soft atmosphere of the fabric. If glass is used, it should be a high quality, reflection free, glass.

We have also mounted batiks occasionally on a circular frame. The batik, of course, has to be specially designed for display in this way. The circle can be cut in either plywood or soft board. The stretching of the fabric is more difficult on this shape of frame, and the cloth should usually be dry cleaned to give it greater elasticity. Again, staple the fabric to the back of the frame, working carefully around the circle to exert equal pressures on all sides of the center of the fabric.

Batiks can often be transformed when a soft light shines through them. If you intend to display the batik in this way, do not dry clean it. When the batik is impregnated with wax, which it is after the partial removal of wax using an iron and absorbent paper, then the colors glow richly when light shines through them. The effect is very similar to that of stained glass. Because of this, batik fabric can be used for startlingly beautiful curtain fabrics and lampshades.

The simplest way to make use of this effect is to prepare the batik as a wall hanging and then hang it in front of some source of light. If a swivel of the type used in a fishing trace is employed in the hanging, and the batik suspended from the ceiling, then it will be free to move around gently in currents of air, catching the light from different directions.

Another way of using light in displaying batik is to construct a frame that will stand on a shelf or table. The batik can be stapled or laced onto the frame and will be visible from all directions.

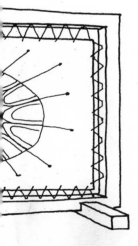

The batik can be laced into a self-supporting frame.

PROJECT IDEAS FOR BATIK

Batik can be used in many ways to enliven the furnishing of a home and to add color to life. In this chapter we suggest some projects that make use of batik fabric in a variety of ways. We have tried to choose simple projects that can be completed with a limited knowledge of needlework and carpentry. The designs are intended as suggestions to spark off your own creative ideas.

Simple Doll

Because batik can be used as a graphic art it is especially suited to the design of soft toys such as animals or dolls which have extensive surface detail. At first choose a relatively simple doll design. The outline of this design is drawn onto some cardboard or stiff paper. This is then cut out and used as a pattern to transfer the outline shape onto two pieces of cotton fabric; one will be the front, the other, the back. If a side view has been chosen, the two pieces will be the two sides. It is better to leave the cutting out of the doll from the fabric until the batik process is finished because a rectangle is easier to deal with than a complicated doll shape, when tacking the fabric down for waxing.

All the features, hair, and clothes can be produced by means of waxing and dyeing. Other items can be used, such as buttons, lace, or wool for hair, to be added after the doll has been batiked. The batik process, however, can be used to produce all these effects. The hair, for example, can be an exciting opportunity to make use of the tjanting. If an appearance of curls and waves is desired, the tjanting is held in contact with the fabric and moved freely over it. Then the whole area is waxed over with a brush. The wax will crack along the tjanting lines and the dye will penetrate these cracks while the hair will remain a fairly uniform color. When dealing with a side-view doll, the simplest way to ensure that both sides correspond, is to double the fabric, which must be a loose, fine cotton. Then when the hot wax is applied it will penetrate both layers of fabric and produce the same design on both.

The clothes, frills, stockings, boots, etc., are treated in much the same way as, for example, the alphabet cushion was done. The tjanting is used for the detailed waxing, the brush is used for the filling in of the colors.

Once the doll fabric is completed and dry cleaned, it is then cut out leaving a seam allowance of about half an inch all round. Put together the outside faces of both halves of the doll (i.e., put the right sides together), and sew up all the way around leaving a smallish opening for stuffing, at the bottom. Turn the doll inside out, and stuff with chosen stuffing. This can be either washed lambs wool, kapok, rags, nylon stockings, dacron filling or sponge pieces. Make sure that the head, neck and arms are well packed before proceeding to the rest of the body. Turn in the raw edges at the bottom, and oversew them together to close the opening.

Pattern for batiked doll, front and back. Many features, hair, eyes, clothing, etc., can be batiked right onto the fabric.

Jointed Doll

Another way of making up the doll would be to use the jointed-doll method. This is more complicated and the design should be kept large to avoid having to sew around small awkward corners. The outline of the doll needs to be drawn onto the fabric as before, but this time one and a half inches must be left between the joints as illustrated in the diagram. When the waxing, dyeing, and removal of the wax is completed the parts of the doll are cut out, leaving about half an inch seam allowance around each piece. Then with right sides together, facing in, sew round the sides of the arms and legs leaving them open at the top. Turn the arms and legs inside out and stuff the arms to the elbow. Sew across the top to close it. Stuff the legs to knees and make sure the feet are pointing forward then sew across the knees. Stuff to the tops of the legs and sew up.

Place the front body in the back body with right sides together on the inside. When sewing leave arm openings and the bottom between the hips, open, plus a small side opening below the waist in the torso. Turn the body right side out. Stuff the head and neck, fit the arms into the arm openings, and sew up. Then stuff the torso to just below the waist. Fit the legs into the body and sew them in. Finish stuffing the body through the small side opening and then turn in the raw edges and oversew. (NOTE: When fitting the arms and legs into the body, the edges of fabric around the openings should also be turned in before the limb is sewn in, to give a neat finish.)

As seen from the illustration this doll is batiked only to give the facial features and some underclothing. So some clothing needs to be made for it. A basic dress can be made in the same way that the first one-piece doll is made. Having designed the dress, a pattern is made, which is used to draw the outline for the front and back onto the fabric. All the necessary detail, such as ribbons, buttons, lace, collar, and patterning is done with batik. The dress is then cut out leaving a half-inch seam allowance all the way around; the shoulders and side seams are sewn up; the edges of the sleeves and the bottom are turned in and hemmed to give a neat finish.

Batiked doll's dress.

Quilted Doll

The quilted doll is more of a decorated motif than a doll. The top layer of fabric only is batiked, the back is left plain. Once again the outline does not want to be too complicated so as to avoid sewing awkward curves. When the batiking is finished lay together the two right sides of the doll, taking no more than the allowance in the seam and leave the bottom edge open. Turn the right side out and stuff lightly so that the layer of stuffing is no deeper than about one and a half inches. Cotton batting or teased out sheep's wool would be

Pattern for the jointed doll. Instead of a dress, the undergarments have been batiked onto the material.

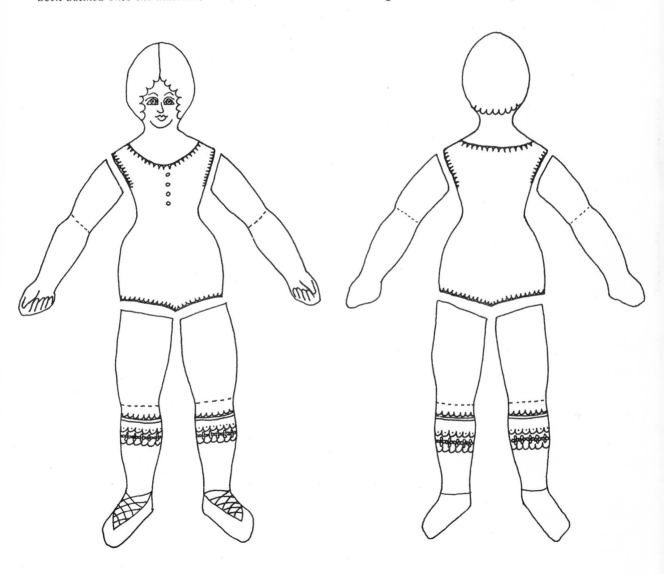

suitable for the stuffing. Close up the bottom by turning the edges and oversewing.

Some lines in the design will be obvious choices for a quilting line, such as round the arm and hand, and around the face. Folds and patterns on the clothing and curls in the hair are other possibilities for quilting lines. The quilting lines can be sewn by machine or by hand; they are sewn right through all three layers.

It would be possible to quilt both sides of a doll before it is made up, in the traditional method of quilting. Then, with right sides together the doll would be made up as described, and the inside of the doll could be stuffed.

Design for a simple quilted doll. In this particular design the dotted lines are possible quilting lines.

Sausage-dog Draft Pillow

A draft excluder is an attractive way of stopping up that gap at the bottom of the door. The body is a long strip—as long as the door for which it is intended is wide. The head should be batiked before it is cut out. The two sides are the same in size and shape but face in opposite directions. The gusset is to give the head shape. The feet and tail are very much just decoration and can be made from a single layer of felt.

After batiking is finished, the body should be made up separately from the head. The body fabric is sewn up along the length with a small stitch or a double line of stitches. The diameter of the two circles that form the two ends of the sausage should be an inch larger than the diameter of the body tube. Before the body is turned right side out, sew one circle onto one end with close, small, tight stitches. Then partially sew the other circle into the other end, leaving an

The sausage-dog draft pillow. The circles are patterns for the ends of the dog, and the triangle shape is the gusset.

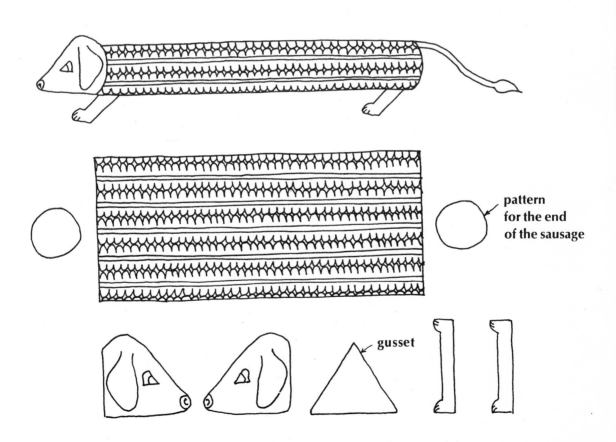

pattern
for the end
of the sausage

gusset

83

opening for stuffing. Turn the body right side out now. It should, ideally, be stuffed with sand, but if the body is not going to be "sand proof," an alternative such as rags can be used. Oversew the opening in the body to close it.

The head is made by sewing the gusset to the lower edge of each of the heads, and then sewing the sides together from the crown of the head to the nose. This should be done with the right sides inside and then turned right side out. Stuff the head and then sew it to the end of the body turning in the raw edges as you proceed. The legs and tail can be fixed on with a few stitches.

Hobbyhorse Head

Hobbyhorse heads are basically made of a stuffed head sewn, stuck, or tied onto a broom handle or a piece of dowel an inch in diameter. They make a versatile toy for a child. The following method combines glueing and sewing for attaching the head to the pole.

Once again the simplest method to transfer the design to the cloth is to cut out a pattern and use it to draw the two sides of the head. When drawing make sure that the two sides are facing in opposite directions. The batiking is straight forward and the patterns can be varied.

Cut out the head and the gusset, leaving a seam allowance of not less than half an inch. Put the batiked side of each side of the head together and pin the gusset into place between the ears. Sew in the gusset and then around the head leaving an opening of about two inches at the base of the head, for the pole. Turn the head right side out and stuff it firmly through the opening.

A strip of fabric measuring about four inches wide by five inches long is now needed for the pole band. To fix the pole band to the pole use an impact adhesive for the glueing. The band should be fixed to the pole about ten to twelve inches from the top of the pole. This will vary with the size of the head, but the pole should extend well up into the head to prevent it becoming too wiggly with use. Having put the glue on the pole, wrap the band around and lap it over on itself. Turn in the raw edge and oversew it to the rest of the band.

Push the pole up into the head and then add some more stuffing around the pole so that it is held firmly. Sew the edges of the opening to the pole band to close it and fix the head in place. The reins can be made of strips of leather, ribbon or tape and they should be attached to each side of the head, at the ring in the halter.

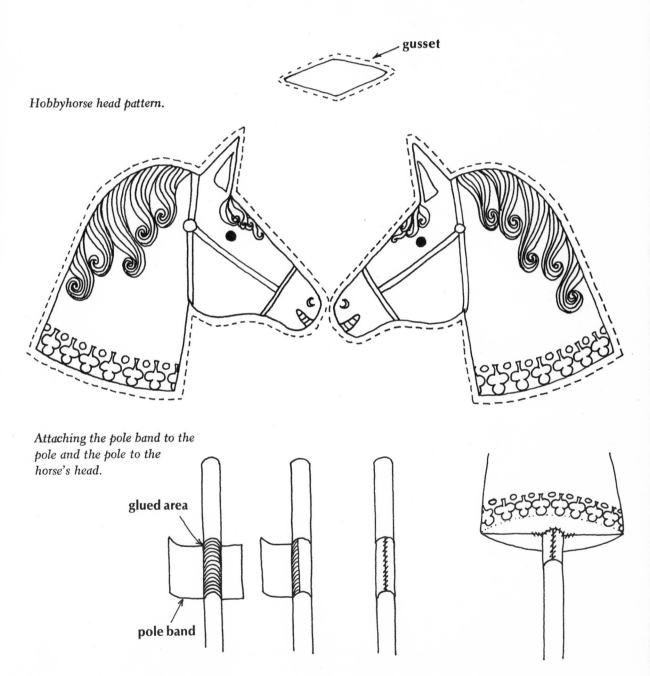

gusset

Hobbyhorse head pattern.

Attaching the pole band to the pole and the pole to the horse's head.

glued area

pole band

Cushions

Pictorial subjects, especially faces, make very interesting batik cushions. The shape of the cushion does not have to be decided before the batik is done; instead the design can be allowed, in its formation, to determine the shape. There is, of course, a limit to how involved the outline can be. Once the batik is finished, the design needs to be cut out leaving the minimum of half an inch seam allowance. The back of the cushion can also be batiked. It can, on the other hand, be left plain. In this case, the fabric chosen can either be in harmony with the colors used in the batik, or in direct contrast with them.

The right sides of the cushion are laid together and it is sewn up leaving an opening for stuffing. The opening is then oversewn to close it. Once again there are a variety of stuffing materials available: cotton batting, wool scraps, sponge pieces, goose down, feathers—even an old cushion can be re-covered in this way.

Patterns for batiked cushions. The dotted lines are the cutting lines.

Room Dividers

Room dividers can be a most spectacular way of using batik because it can be done on a large scale and enough light can shine through the fabric to make the colors come alive.

With a single layer of fabric, a fairly simple floor to ceiling divider can be made using techniques for the stretching of the fabric similar to those described in the chapter on Framing.

The supporting skeleton for the divider is made up of a wall post, an end post, a top rail, and a bottom rail. The end post should be one-and-a-half-inches thick, but the rest of the wood can be three-quarters-of-an-inch or an inch thick. The width is a personal choice; between four to six inches is the most suitable. Position the divider to correspond to the ceiling joists, if possible, because it makes the construction so much easier. The ceiling joists and wall studs are usually sixteen inches apart, and can be found by tapping the wall and listening to the difference between the hollow and the solid sounds.

First prepare the wall post to the full height of the room, then notch it to take the top and bottom rails. The rails and end post are cut and notched in the same manner. If the wall is brick, drill and plug, then screw the wall post into position. If the wall has wooden studs they will correspond to the ceiling joists, so screw the wall post directly into the wall stud. The top rail is fitted into the notch in the wall post and screwed into the ceiling joist. The bottom rail is also fitted into the notch in the wall post and then screwed into the floor boards. The end post is fitted up against the ends of the top and bottom rails and nailed into them.

The batik needs to be stretched onto a frame, the outside measurement of which is three to four inches smaller than the inside of the divider, *on all sides*. The stretcher could be made of a simple mitered rectangle using wood measuring one inch by two inches. The batik is then stapled onto the outside edge of the frame, instead of onto the back. Four mitered strips of one-quarter-inch thick wood are then nailed round the outside edge of the batik, thus covering the raw edges and giving a neat finish.

This frame can now be fixed into position inside the divider. Cut eight lengths of one-inch-diameter dowling three

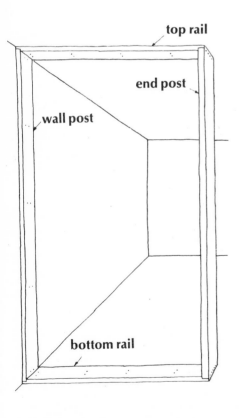

top rail

end post

wall post

bottom rail

The frame for a divider.

and a half inches long. (This length will depend on the difference in size between the "skeleton" of the divider and the framed batik.) Drill right through each length of dowling to allow for the easy passage of an eight- or ten-diameter screw. Drill through the top, bottom, and sides of the batik frame and countersink on the inside edge of the frame. It is then a simple matter to screw through the frame and dowling into the top, bottom rails, and side posts using a five-and-a-half or six-inch-long screw.

The fabric for such a large item would have to be waxed a small area at a time. It is important that the area is as near to the hot wax as possible. Particularly when using the brush, the wax must not be allowed to cool on the brush before it reaches the fabric. A large table is a help and the fabric, during each waxing, needs to be rotated so that the area being waxed is close to the wax pot. A large receptacle is necessary for the dyeing; a bathtub can make a very successful dye vat.

Still on the theme of room dividers, a hinged screen can

Stretching the batik over the wooden frame that is three to four inches smaller than the inside of the divider.

also be a vehicle for batik. Each section can be part of a large design which is divided after the batiking process, bearing in mind that some of the fabric must be used up when it is stretched and a continuous motif could be spoiled unless the placing of the dividing lines along which it will be cut is kept in mind. The batik for each section can also be made separately with, perhaps, a unifying theme in mind.

Light and semitransparent fabrics can be used in layers of two or more, allowing the batik on each layer to be superimposed on the other layers. When moving past such an arrangement there is an interesting effect of movement between the superimposed designs. A large boxlike frame with a transparent batik set into each side, will give this effect. Another possibility is to hang a number of lengths from the ceiling. Each length is fixed to a rod and each rod is hung from the ceiling, a few inches apart. The fabric will waft gently in the breezes and the light will combine the design on each to give a whole effect.

*Pieces of wooden dowels are
then used to hold the batik inside
the frame of the room divider.*

Three other room divider ideas.

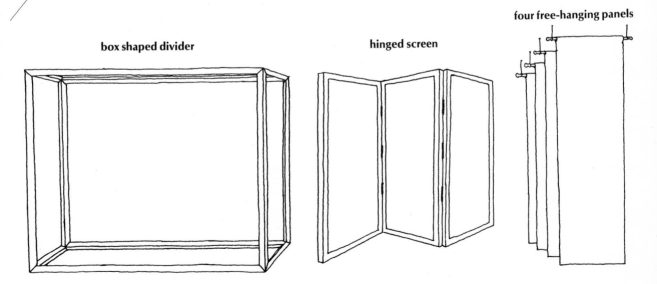

box shaped divider   **hinged screen**   **four free-hanging panels**

Lampshades

Making lampshades of batiked materials is another opportunity to give the colors that brilliance that light shining through in a diffused way can give. A good quality cotton with a close weave will give the best effects.

A simple lampshade can be made using a straight sided frame. Frames come in almost any shape or size, but the easiest to use and the best for showing off the batik are those with straight, or almost straight, sides. The methods whereby the shade is fixed to the stand or light bulb vary, too, and can be chosen to best suit the purpose of the light as a whole.

Using a straight-sided round frame with a swivel gimbal for attachment, the cloth is cut to be just a little bigger than the circumference of the frame with two inches extra at the top and bottom. When the batik is completed put the right sides together and stitch up the short side making a tube of the fabric. A hem is then made around the top and bottom circumference through which elastic is threaded and tied loosely enough to enable it to be fitted over the frame. Once the fabric is on the frame the elastic can be pulled tighter to stretch it taut over the frame.

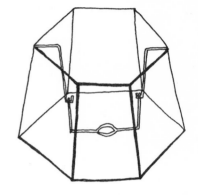

A more complicated type of shade that can be made to good effect with batiked fabric is the pleated shade. A soft fabric is the most suitable, and silk would be excellent both in terms of the lampshade and the batik.

The frame to use is one with fixed struts (the uprights that connect the upper circle to the lower circle) and a bigger circle at the bottom than at the top. The metal frame must be covered entirely with tape, with the exception of the filament (the part of the frame that is used for attachment to the stand). The reasons for taping is to cover up the bumps of the welded joints, to give something to sew the fabric to and to hide the metal, which in a shade of this nature is more easily seen and can spoil the effect.

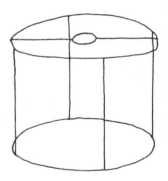

Half-inch white tape is the best; it is cheap, strong, easy to sew into, and can easily be dyed any color. It is usual to cover the downward struts first, and the horizontal rings last. The amount of tape necessary can be calculated with the following formula. The struts need one and a half times their length; the rings need four and a half times their diameter.

Cut a length for the first strut and fold about three

Different style lampshades.

90

Taping the metal frame of the pleated lampshade to cover up rough edges, and hide the metal.

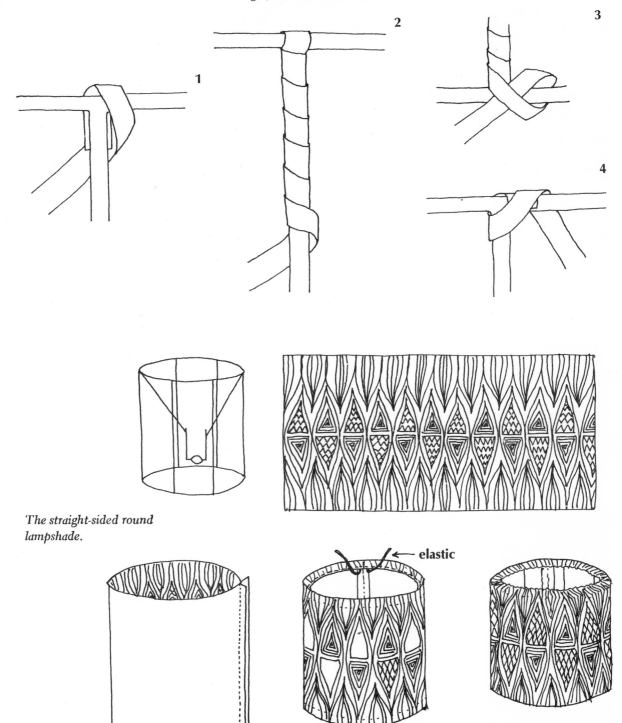

The straight-sided round lampshade.

← **elastic**

quarters of an inch over the top of the strut, holding it in place with one hand while the other hand binds it into place with the remaining length. Wind the tape diagonally down the strut, overlapping each layer slightly. Pull the tape firmly after each wind so that the whole binding effect is tight and will not unravel. At the bottom of the strut, take the tape over and under the base of the frame and bring the end through the loop thus formed. Pull the end very tight and leave it dangling.

When all but one of the downward struts have been covered, cut one length of tape long enough to cover the top ring, the last strut *and* the bottom ring. Fold the end of the tape round the strut and along the top ring. Wrap it into place and continue around the top ring, then down the last strut and around the bottom ring. When the binding is complete pin the final end into position and stitch firmly so that the stitching will be covered by the shade.

Once the frame is taped it should be dipped into a dye bath of the dominant color used in the batik, then rinsed and dried. The silk should be cut on the straight, equal in length to the circumference of the bottom of the frame plus one inch overlap. With the wrong side of the material outwards and hanging below the edge of the frame, turn the short edge back about half an inch and pin the long edge onto the bottom of the frame starting at a strut. The turning should be held in place with the pin. Pin every half an inch attaching the silk to the tape. Pull fabric tight as pinning proceeds.

With close oversewing stitches, sew the silk to the tape round the bottom ring of the frame. Where the last short side overlaps the first folded edge, make a neat flat seam right down the material. Trim the raw edges around the bottom of the frame. Pull the silk up the frame so that it becomes the right side out and covers the frame. Mark the top edge of the fabric to divide it into equal sections to correspond to the number of struts. Attach the fabric to each strut at each dividing mark. Make even pleats in the material between each strut and pin each pleat to the top ring. Stitch these pleats to the tape with close oversewing stitches. Turn surplus fabric over to the outside of the frame; lash it down with long stitches; then cut off the surplus close to these lashing stitches. Cover top and bottom edges of the shade with trimming using a fast drying waterproof glue. This gives a neat finish and covers the raw edge at the top of the shade.

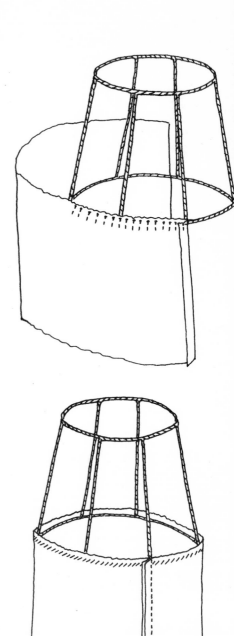

Attaching the fabric to the bottom ring of the lampshade.

Quilts

The alphabet-cushion design would make an effective design for a child's quilt because incorporated into the design are the natural lines for the quilting lines. The circus design also lends itself to this kind of thing, being made up of a number of motifs.

The muslin for the top and underside can be cut to the approximate size needed, depending on the size of the bed for which it is intended. When estimating the yardage, it must first be decided if the quilt is to cover only the top of the bed or if it is to hang down on each side like a bedspread. Also, some allowance must be made for the padding effect, which will take up a little extra fabric. Sixty inches wide by seventy-eight inches would be large enough to cover a single bed like a bedspread.

For the circus design the divisions between each motif are marked on the fabric as a guide for batiking. The color combinations for each motif must be basically the same because the fabric is dipped into the dye as a whole. For each color the whole piece is waxed, each motif, at the same time. It is possible to omit a color from one motif while including it into others, by not waxing over that color in one particular area.

Once the batiked sheet is completed place it over the quilt batting with the lining muslin underneath that. These three layers can be pinned together to prevent slipping. Cut three-inch strips of contrasting fabric and press under the edges to form one-and-a-half-inch strips. These strips are then pinned onto the top of the batiked muslin to cover the joins or junctions between each motif in the design. Stitch along the edges of the strips, through all three layers. This can be done by hand or by machine, and both edges of the strip must be sewn down. For the border of the quilt, the same contrasting fabric can be used. It should be cut wide enough to overlap the edges on both sides, top, and bottom.

These border strips are sewn together by mitering the corners for a neat finish. Press under the seam allowance on the inside edges of the border. Fit the edges of the quilt into this folded border and sew along the inside edge of the strip through the five thicknesses of fabric to the edge of the border underneath. This technique is similar to that of putting blanket ribbon around a blanket.

Costumes

The fabric can be cut out in a simple basic pattern to open down the back, with long or short sleeves. The body section can be adjusted in length to suit the purpose. A paper pattern can be made using the adult or child for whom the costume is intended, and this pattern is then used to cut out the fabric. The pieces of fabric should be batiked before the garment is sewn. The shoulder and center front seams are sewn first and then the sleeves are set in. The sleeve seam and side seam are sewn all in one. Neaten all the raw edges by turning in once and stitching. The back may be fastened in a variety of ways; ties are perhaps the easiest.

For this, batik is used to produce all the detail of the costume so eliminate from the sewing process collars, buttons, lapels, badges, aprons, pockets, and waistcoats (vests), etc. The idea can also be used for trousers, headdresses, and cloaks.

Batiked costumes.

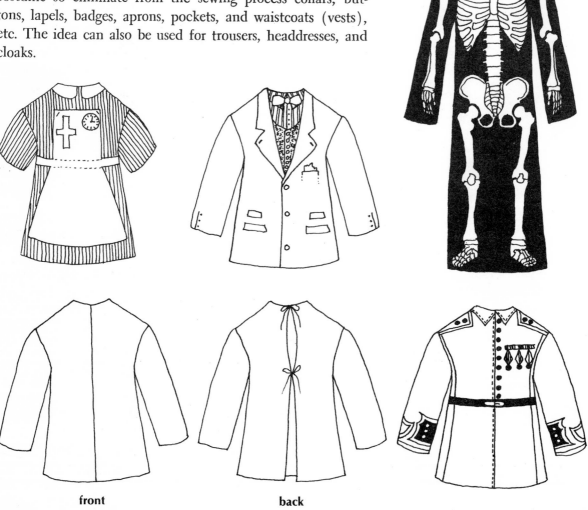

front   back

DYEING CHART

	red	orange	yellow	green	blue	purple	brown	gray
red	red	orangy red	orange	brown	purple	wine	reddish	reddish
orange	orangy red	orange	yellowy orange	brown	brown	reddish brown	golden brown	olive green
yellow	orange	yellowy orange	yellow	chartreuse (yellowy green)	green	brown	yellowish brown	sage green
green	brown	brown	yellowy green	green	turquoise	brown	greenish brown	greeny gray
blue	purple	brown	green	turquoise	blue	deep purple	dark brown	darker blue
purple	wine	reddish brown	brown	brown	deep purple	purple	reddish brown	dark purple
brown	reddish brown	golden brown	yellowish brown	greenish brown	dark gray	reddish brown	brown	dark gray
gray	reddish brown	olive green	sage green	greeny gray	dark blue (dull)	dark purple	dark brown	gray

SUPPLIES AND BOOKS TO READ

SOME OTHER BOOKS ON BATIK

Batik, Tony Bachem-Heinen (New York: Herder and Herder, 1969).

Batik: Art and Craft, Nik Kreritsky (Reinhold, New York: 1966).

Batik the Art and Craft, Ila Keller (Rutland, Vermont: Charles Tuttle and Company, 1966).

The Book of Batik, Ernst Muhling (New York: Taplinger, 1967).

Introducing Batik, Evelyn Samuel (New York: Watson-Guptill, 1968).

Batik as a Hobby, Vivian Stein (New York: Sterling Publishing Company, 1969).

LIST OF SUPPLIERS

The following are among the major suppliers in the United States of America who have a mail order business:

Aiko's Art Materials Import, 714 Wabash Avenue, Chicago, Illinois 60611. Wide range of supplies including three ranges of dyes, traditional and modern tools and materials.

Artis, 9123 East Las Tunas, Temple City, California 91780. Supply materials and Lejeune Dyes for batik.

Bergen Arts and Crafts, 35 Congress Street, Salem, Massachusetts 01970. Good range of tools and materials for batik, including cold-water dyes for silk and cotton.

Craftool, 1 Industrial Road, Woodbridge, New Jersey 07075. Markets tools and dyes for batik and a batik kit.

W. Cushing and Company, Dover-Foxcroft, Maine 04426. Manufacture and distribute Cushing's Perfection Dyes, the dyes used by the authors in their batiks.

Durable Arts, P. O. Box 2413, San Rafael, California 94901. Batik dyes and materials under Versatex trademark.

Fezandie and Sperrie, 103 Lafayette Street, New York, New York 10013. Dyes only. Wide range available in various quantities especially formulated for batik.

Sam Flax, 25 East 28th Street, New York, New York 10016 and 551 Madison Avenue, New York, New York 10022.

Magnus Craft Materials, 109 Lafayette Street, New York, New York 10013.

Michaels Artist and Engineering, 7005 Tijuaga Avenue, North Hollywood, California 91605.

New York Central Supply, 62 Third Avenue, New York, New York 10003.

Screen Process Supplies, 1199 East 12th Street, Oakland, California 94606. Suppliers of Inko dye and tools and materials for batik.